LESSONS FROM OUR FAILURE TO BUILD A CONSTITUTIONAL BRIDGE IN THE 2023 REFERENDUM

FRANK BRENNAN

connorcourt
PUBLISHING

Other books by Frank Brennan

CONNOR COURT PUBLISHING PTY LTD
PO Box 7257
Redland Bay QLD 4165
sales@connorcourt.com
www.connorcourtpublishing.com.au

ISBN 9781923224124

Cover design by Ian James.

Front cover painting: The Bridge in-curve (1930), Grace Cossington SMITH.
© Estate of Grace Cossington Smith

The portrait on the back cover by Mary Larnach Jones was commissioned by Newman
College at the University of Melbourne at the conclusion of Frank's term as Rector.

Dedicated to

Dr Lowitja O'Donoghue AC CBE DSG (1932-2024)

who told us:

'We cannot lose the will to resolve these issues, because they will
not go away.
But tackling them half-heartedly or high-handedly will be a recipe
for continuing failure.
I believe that solutions are at hand.
But they will require determination and patient effort,
negotiation and compromise,
imagination and true generosity.'

Contents

Foreword

Mr John Lochowiak

Chairperson of the National Aboriginal and Torres Strait Islander Catholic Council

I am honoured to have been asked to write this foreword for *Lessons from Our Failure to Build a Constitutional Bridge in the 2023 Referendum.*

I am also honoured to consider Fr Frank a friend, not only to me, but also to my Aboriginal and Torres Strait Islander brothers and sisters. In fact, he has been adopted – Aboriginal way – into our family, making him a 'Brother'. He has worked tirelessly over many, many years, following not only in the footsteps of his father, Sir Gerard Brennan, but his fellow Jesuits who are also committed to justice and equality in our country.

Obviously, the referendum journey was a challenging one. We felt the highs of the initial announcements and ultimately the lows of an historic defeat of a modest, albeit imperfect call from Australia's First Peoples to be heard by our leaders. Aboriginal and Torres Strait Islander people are now in the process of healing our spirit.

Throughout the journey, Fr Frank and I produced resources, presented side by side and spoke at length about our hopes and concerns. Testament to his respect for our First Peoples, he acknowledged very early in the piece that the Catholic Church needed to listen to our National Aboriginal and Torres Strait Islander Catholic Council (NATSICC). He embodied this belief by paying as deep regard to my thoughts as an Aboriginal man as I did to his as an expert on the Constitution and the Law.

Something we always discussed were the 'What ifs' – What if it gets up? What if it fails? We always knew that the day of the Referendum was a starting point, not an end point. It is now time to unpack what happened and take lessons from both sides of the argument, with an eye to the future.

This book casts a critical eye on the processes and resulting failure to create a national 'theatre' for respectful dialogue between two opposing, and valid points of view. Whilst I know that I will never see another referendum in my lifetime, I hope that my children will have the opportunity to participate fully in decisions that affect them and all First Australians, having learnt from the failings of their forbears.

These discussions form a part of the healing that needs to happen in families, friendship groups and communities. At NATSICC, we remain hopeful, always hopeful, that we will have input to decisions, projects and initiatives that will improve the lives of our people.

I commend to you *Lessons from Our Failure to Build a Constitutional Bridge in the 2023 Referendum,* because we must all assume a role in shaping our Great Southern Land heeding the lessons from the past.

Introduction

The result of the 2023 referendum on the Voice was a disaster for the country and a tragedy for First Australians. A week after the 40:60 loss, the key Indigenous leaders who had dealt with the Albanese government during the campaign broke their silence and issued a powerful statement saying:

> 'Aboriginal and Torres Strait Islander peoples are in shock and are grieving the result. We feel acutely the repudiation of our peoples and the rejection of our efforts to pursue reconciliation in good faith. That people who came to our country in only the last 235 years would reject the recognition of this continent's First Peoples – on our sacred land which we have cared for and nurtured for more than 65,000 years – is so appalling and mean-spirited as to be utterly unbelievable a week following. It will remain unbelievable and appalling for decades to come.'[1]

There has been little appetite for public discussion about lessons to be learnt from this abject failure. Some of the key proponents saw nothing wrong with the process and nothing wrong with the wording of the proposed change. They think that racism played a key part in the result. For example, the key Indigenous leaders claimed, 'It is clear no reform of the Constitution that includes our peoples will ever succeed. This is the bitter lesson from 14 October.'[2] If they're right, there will be no point in attempting again constitutional recognition of First Australians. But they may be wrong – and I hope they are. There may be a prospect of future constitutional change but not with the process that was adopted and not with the wording that was proposed in 2023. It's time to begin the conversation about past mistakes, before we all start forgetting what went on.

During the course of the Voice campaign, I published three editions of my book *An Indigenous Voice to Parliament: Seeking a Constitutional Bridge*.[3] I had spent two years as a member of the Senior Advisory Group appointed by the Morrison Government on the co-design of the Voice. We were led by Aboriginal leaders Professors Marcia Langton and Tom Calma. Earlier, I had been privileged to be asked by Dr Lowitja O'Donoghue to deliver the 2017 Lowitja Oration marking the 50th anniversary of the 1967 referendum. During 2023, I was commissioned by the Jesuit Provincial to conduct the Jesuits' Bookends project, being a resource for First Nations and church groups wanting a better understanding of the issues at play in the referendum. I gave many talks the length and breadth of the country. In every audience there were rusted on yes voters and committed no voters. But there were also those who were undecided and genuinely concerned to cast a vote that would make a real and positive change for First Nations' people and the nation.

In 2015, I had published a book *No Small Change: The Road to Recognition for Indigenous Australia*[4], arguing two propositions. I thought the lesson of the 1967 referendum was that the Australian people were open to giving overwhelming support to a constitutional change which could be described as minimal and symbolic, and that such a change carried overwhelmingly provided the impetus for significant policy change and legal enhancement of Indigenous rights – moving the country from assimilation to self determination, and from terra nullius to land rights. I thought a second referendum for a minimal symbolic change carried overwhelmingly could once again provide further impetus for substantive legal and policy changes.

I was convinced from the outset that no referendum could succeed without bipartisan support in our Parliament. To have any chance of attracting such support, it was necessary to have the process right and to have the proposed wording of the amendment right. I thought the Albanese government got both wrong from the beginning.

Now that the 2023 referendum is well behind us, I think it would be useful to publish my main post-Voice reflections as well as papers I prepared during the campaign dealing with concerns about process and wording. I make no pretence to have got everything right during the campaign. But it is in the interests of all those wanting to learn lessons from the past to have maximum access to the various competing viewpoints at play in 2023. It's this variety of viewpoints which would have been aired if there had been a constitutional convention or a transparent parliamentary committee process for bringing all parties to the table and winning overall acceptance of a formula of words with minimal legal uncertainty.

The Albanese government decided to forego a constitutional convention. And by the time they announced the setting up of a parliamentary committee process, the proposed wording of the constitutional amendment was already set in stone. One of my major concerns was the breadth of the constitutional entitlement of the Voice to make representations not just on proposed laws and policies, but on routine administrative decisions by public servants whenever a decision was to be made relating to any Aboriginal or Torres Strait Islander persons. In administrative law, if a person has an entitlement to make a representation to a public servant making a decision about matters relating to the person, there is an entitlement to receive adequate notice and adequate information so as to allow the making of a reasoned representation. I thought such a constitutional entitlement could bog down our system of government, reducing, rather than enhancing, government's capacity to 'close the gap'. Some argued that the Parliament could limit the extent to which these representations could be made. But there was strong disagreement amongst some of the nation's leading lawyers.

In this book, I provide not only my post-Voice reflections but also the formal representations I made to government seeking an improvement of process and wording.

For the more technically minded, I also provide the five notes on justiciability that I circulated last year during the referendum campaign addressing the issue of representations being made to public servants and government entities on all manner of things which might relate to Aboriginal and Torres Strait Islander citizens.

The major challenge for the country in the future will be according First Australians agency and self-determination while remaining true to the undoubted rules for constitutional change. Indigenous leaders will not accept minimal symbolic change to the Constitution. It will be necessary to find that sweet spot of substantive change acceptable to most members of the Commonwealth Parliament. There may be one, but there may not. Finding it will take great trust and collaboration. This is my modest contribution to the necessary conversation which, sadly, will take another generation.

1

Post-Referendum Reflections

Homily the Morning After the Referendum[5]

This morning, I call to mind the Aboriginal woman who spoke at the end of a forum we held in Darwin on the Voice. She told us: 'A lot of my people don't understand all the law and politics about this Voice. All I know is that when they wake up on Sunday 15 October and if the answer is NO, they will think that they have been rejected once again by the people who dispossessed and colonised them without their consent.' She wept. We all shed a tear.

May our Aboriginal brothers and sisters be consoled by the words in today's first reading from Isaiah:[6]

> On this mountain the LORD of hosts
> will provide for all peoples
> a feast of rich food and choice wines,
> juicy, rich food and pure, choice wines.
> On this mountain he will destroy
> the veil that veils all peoples,
> the web that is woven over all nations;
> he will destroy death forever.
> The Lord GOD will wipe away
> the tears from every face;
> the reproach of his people he will remove

from the whole earth; for the LORD has spoken.
On that day it will be said:
'Behold our God, to whom we looked to save us!
This is the LORD for whom we looked;
let us rejoice and be glad that he has saved us!'
For the hand of the LORD will rest on this mountain.

The people have spoken, and very clearly. The answer is a resounding NO. No matter how any of us voted, we need to respect the will of the people. We need to accept the decision. Despite our differences, we need to come together and address the unfinished business of our history and of our governance arrangements which are failing to close the gap. We need to find a new pathway for closing the gap, acknowledging the place of First Australians.

There's no doubt that the Prime Minister gave it his all. There will be plenty of debate in the coming days about whether he and his advisers followed the best processes and settled on the best proposal. A homily is no place for allocating political blame. Suffice to say that there was not enough common ground between Messrs Albanese and Dutton to bring the country to YES in the numbers needed to amend the Australian Constitution.

The NO vote is not indicative of a racist or stupid nation. It is the sure sign that we the people were not presented with a proposal for change to the Constitution sufficiently safe and certain to win the support of the vast majority of politicians in our parliament. And thus it was not a proposal likely to win the support of the voters. No referendum has ever succeeded without support from all major political parties. The Labor Party has always been more adventurous than the conservative parties seeking constitutional change on all manner of things. They have now made 26 attempts to amend the

Constitution. This is their 25th failed attempt.

There were eloquent Aboriginal voices for YES and eloquent Aboriginal voices for NO. No wonder so many voters were left wondering if the proposed Voice would divide the nation or not; whether it would help to close the gap or not; and whether it would clog the workings of government or not.

Some who voted YES thought the proposed change was perfect, certain and workable. Others of us thought the words imperfect, but far preferred a change to the Constitution with imperfect words rather than no change to the Constitution whatever. We thought the matter had been left unresolved for too long, and could not see how it would be resolved any better in the foreseeable future. But it was not to be.

This referendum was nothing like the 1967 referendum. It was nothing like the same sex marriage plebiscite. In 1967, over 90% of voters supported a proposal put forward by all members of our parliament urging that Aboriginal people be treated the same as the rest of us. In the same sex marriage plebiscite, over 60% of those who chose to vote supported a proposal that the civil institution of marriage be made available to all couples regardless of their sexual orientation. In both these votes, we were voting to treat everyone the same.

This referendum was nothing of the sort. In fact, it was probably the exact opposite. On one reading, the 60% NO vote was a decision once again to treat everyone the same, declining to set up a new constitutional entity available only to one group of citizens, namely the First Australians.

Without a people's convention and without a parliamentary

supervised process inviting citizens to honest, transparent dialogue about the structure and purpose of a Voice, we were setting up the referendum to fail.

Many Australians with an Aboriginal heritage still suffer the effects of past dispossession and colonisation. The statistics speak for themselves. There is more we need to do to correct their continuing poverty, disadvantage and dispossession. When it comes to the Constitution, the unresolved question is whether those Australians with an Aboriginal heritage should be specifically recognised, not because they are poor, disadvantaged or dispossessed, but because they are the First Australians. Imagine that the time was to come when most Aboriginal Australians were no longer poor, disadvantaged and dispossessed. Would there still be a need to make special provision for them in the Constitution? Many of us think that the answer to that question is YES, and we can invoke many statements by recent popes to support that position. But the majority of our fellow citizens still need to be convinced that any permanent special provision should be more than minimal, symbolic recognition.

After the Mabo decision in 1992, I was addressing a group of lawyers. At the end of my presentation, one lawyer introduced himself: 'My name is Murphy. If you are going to have special rights for the Aboriginal people, why not have special rights for the Irish?' I answered, 'Being a Brennan and my mother an O'Hara, I have considerable sympathy for the rights of the Irish. But I think the relevant comparison is not with the Irish in Australia, but with the Irish in Ireland. Though living on the other side of the globe, I take some delight in the thought that there is somewhere on God's earth where the Irish can be as Irish as they like, as well or badly as they can, as selfishly or selflessly as they will. That's just the way the Irish do it.' I continued: 'There is only one place on earth where Aboriginal people can be as Aboriginal as they like, and that's here in the Land of the Holy Spirit, Australia. They may be only 3% of the population, but surely we have to provide for them to maintain their heritage and their culture as best they can in the modern post-colonial world of modern Australia.'

It will be another generation before we revisit the recognition of the First Australians in the Constitution. Let's hope that we have done a better job by then convincing our fellow citizens that there will always be a need for some special laws and policies to be made for the First Australians and that it is unthinkable that such laws be made without some assurance that they will be adequately consulted. That assurance should be part of our Constitution.

Holding in our hearts the many Aboriginal and Torres Strait Islander people who will be feeling rejected this morning, we recall those words of Pope John Paul II at Alice Springs in 1986:

> 'If you stay closely united, you are like a tree standing in the middle of a bush-fire sweeping through the timber. The leaves are scorched and the tough bark is scarred and burned; but inside the tree the sap is still flowing, and under the ground the roots are still strong. Like that tree you have endured the flames, and you still have the power to be reborn. The time for this rebirth is now!'[7]

The Weekend Australian

21 October 2023[8]

Room must be made at the table for other Indigenous voices

At the Prime Minister's news conference acknowledging the loss of the referendum last Saturday night, a journalist asked : 'Why do you think Australians voted No?' Mr. Albanese's answer could not have been simpler: 'The analysis will go on for some time, no doubt. But the truth is that no referendum has succeeded in this country without bipartisan support. None.'[9]

There's really not much need for further analysis than that. We all knew that from Day One. Putting his all into his bold election commitment to implement the Uluru Statement in full, the Prime Minister thought it worth a shot without bipartisan support. Many of us were not convinced, with Labor having lost 24 of the 25 referendum proposals it had put up since federation.

In February this year, seven months after the Prime Minister's Garma announcement and six weeks before the parliamentary committee was finally set up calling the Coalition to the table, I had suggested a way forward to some Coalition members. Liberal Party frontbencher Dan Tehan responded: 'We need a process to achieve a bipartisan outcome and nothing is being offered. It is take it or leave it at the moment. It is not clear who we are negotiating with, so who do we put our common ground to? We have stated very clearly we support Indigenous recognition in the Constitution. That should be the starting point. The government won't even state clearly if the Calma/Langton report is their agreed approach. A detail-lite approach to constitutional change is making it very hard to start consensus building let alone to reach agreement.'[10]

By April, the horse had bolted. There was never a timely, transparent process for the building of bipartisanship. There was no constitutional convention. There was no parliamentary process put in place until the words were set in stone. The key Liberal 'Yes' voter Andrew Bragg rightly described the belated parliamentary process as 'a joke'. The referendum was doomed.

Bipartisanship has always been a necessary precondition, and always will be. It wouldn't matter what the topic of any referendum. It's immaterial who was mostly to blame this time. Some will lay most of the blame at the feet of Albanese. Others, at the feet of Dutton. Most people will allocate blame according to their party political preference. Australians will not vote to change the Constitution unless the major political parties are on board.

Now is the time to move on.

It's been common ground since 2007 there is a need for some form of recognition of Aboriginal and Torres Strait Islander peoples in the Constitution. We've blown that chance for another generation.

It's common ground too that the 'Closing the Gap' statistics are a national disgrace. More needs to be done to deliver appropriate services and opportunities to people living in remote communities.

And it's common ground better outcomes are achieved when services and opportunities are tailored to the needs and desires of those living in remote communities. There is a need for remote voices to be heard.

During the referendum debate, we heard little about the Coalition of Peaks which 'comprises nearly every national, state and territory Aboriginal and Torres Strait Islander community-controlled peak organisation'. It's time for the Albanese Labor Government to put its own stamp on the National Agreement on Closing the Gap, which came into effect three years ago under the Morrison Government.

Much of the referendum debate was focused on health needs in remote communities. But we heard little about NACCHO, the National Aboriginal Community Controlled Health Organisation. During the referendum debate, the Health Minister Mark Butler wrote an opinion piece for *The Australian* on the Voice without even mentioning NACCHO or the Coalition of Peaks. He said: 'A voice to the parliament and, frankly, to the health minister, whether they're Labor or Liberal, is a chance to turn a new page in our national efforts to close the gap.'[11] In the absence of a constitutional Voice, presumably more could be done to ensure that the Coalition of Peaks and NACCHO have a place at the table whenever the Health Minister is considering Indigenous health issues aimed at closing the gap.

Hearing the government ministers during the referendum debate, one could have been forgiven for thinking that the many advisory bodies currently in place did not exist, or that they were not listened to by ministers and senior public servants in Canberra, or that they gave useless advice. Maybe these bodies can be improved. Maybe it's time to audit the performance of the many advisory bodies and better co-ordinate their access to government and to the Parliament by means of the parliamentary committee processes.

It's time also to confront where there is not common ground in the Australian community. We have absolutely no agreement on the issue of equality under the law. Most of those voters who voted 'No' thought a constitutional Voice would divide the nation because the Constitution should treat everyone the same. We Australians are not alone wrestling with this issue of equality. It has three aspects. To what extent should we allow positive discrimination in favour of citizens who together with their ancestors have suffered acute injustice? To what extent should we make special provision for those who rightly claim an Indigenous heritage? To what extent should we recognise perpetual, collective rights rather than individual rights which might be supplemented by temporary special measures to address disadvantage?

Though we do not have a bill of rights, we can often learn from the jurisprudence of the US Supreme Court when considering these three questions. While we were engaged in our referendum debate, the US Supreme Court delivered key decisions on equal protection for African Americans and on the ongoing recognition of the distinctive rights of American Indians.

In a 6-3 decision, the court struck down the admissions scheme for Harvard University which allowed consideration to be given to an applicant's African American heritage. It's useful to consider the passionate disagreement between the two African American judges on the court. Justice Jackson, the newest member of the court and a member of the minority, said: 'Gulf-sized race-based gaps exist with respect to the health, wealth, and well-being of American citizens. They were created in the distant past, but have indisputably been passed down to the present day through the generations. Every moment these gaps persist is a moment in which this great country falls short of actualizing one of its foundational principles—the "self-evident" truth that all of us are created equal.'[12] She proclaimed, 'Our country has never been colorblind.'[13]

Justice Thomas, the court's longest serving judge and a member of the majority, retorted: 'Justice Jackson's race-infused world view falls flat at each step. Individuals are the sum of their unique experiences, challenges, and accomplishments. What matters is not the barriers they face, but how they choose to confront them. And their race is not to blame for everything—good or bad—that happens in their lives. A contrary, myopic world view based on individuals' skin color to the total exclusion of their personal choices is nothing short of racial determinism.'[14]

This is also an unresolved debate for us in Australia. The conflict over this issue was one aspect of the toxic referendum debate. Invoking an earlier decision of the Supreme Court, Chief Justice Roberts, another member of the majority, wrote: 'Our acceptance of race-based state action has been rare for a reason. Distinctions between citizens solely because of their ancestry are by their very nature odious to a free people whose institutions are founded upon the doctrine of equality. That principle cannot be overridden except in the most extraordinary case.'[15]

But even Chief Justice Roberts would admit one extraordinary case, that is the case of native Americans. In the same month as the Harvard decision, the court delivered judgment in two cases relating to native Americans. In one of those cases, the court by 7 to 2 upheld the *Indian Child Welfare Act* which gave preference to the choice of the tribe when deciding where to place a child for adoption even though the state authorities had decided that an alternative arrangement would be in the best interests of the child.

Justice Amy Coney Barrett, one of the most conservative justices on the court who has adopted two children from Haiti, wrote for six of the judges upholding the tribe's collective right to determine such matters in the interests of the tribe. Reviewing the court's consistent jurisprudence on Indian rights, Barrett wrote: 'The trust relationship between the United States and the Indian people informs the exercise of legislative power. As we have explained, the Federal Government has charged itself with moral obligations of the highest responsibility and trust toward Indian tribes. This Court has recognized the distinctive obligation of trust incumbent upon the Government in its dealings with these dependent and sometimes exploited people.'[16]

Most Australians would accept in the wake of the Mabo decision that it is right and proper that special laws provide for the communal native title rights of the First Australians. The referendum result demonstrates that most Australians are yet to accept that there is a case for constitutionalising any collective Aboriginal entitlement, even the modest entitlement to have a Voice making representations on matters relating to them.

We of the present generation have blown the one chance we had to recognise Aboriginal and Torres Strait Islander peoples in the Constitution, and on terms acceptable to them. We have it within our power now to enhance the delivery of services and opportunities to First Australians by having our Parliament and government listen to them more attentively and resource them more efficiently. It will be for the next generation to improve our understanding of equality under the law – putting right past injustices, recognising distinctive Indigenous rights, and determining whether permanent collective rights have any place in our Constitution. It was unreal to expect that these matters could be resolved during a partisan referendum debate in which either Mr Albanese or Mr Dutton was to be blamed and branded a loser.

A week after the election of the Albanese government, I said that the only formula for constitutional change to win approval from the Australian people would be one approved by Noel Pearson and John Howard. We await the new generation of leaders to take the baton and lead the nation on the unfinished business of constitutional recognition of the First Australians. Meanwhile much needs to be done and can be done to address present concerns while the Constitution remains unamended for another generation.

Interview with Kieran Gilbert
23 October 2023[17]

KG: Joining me now is Jesuit priest and law professor Father Frank Brennan, an advocate for Indigenous rights over many decades. He joins me now. Father Frank, no referendum has succeeded in our history without bipartisan support, without bipartisanship in our political system. You have said that and warned the government and the yes campaign on that very point for many months, but sadly you weren't listen to.

FB: Well I'm not the only one who wasn't listen to Kieran. But it is a self-evident fact of Australian political history. Just listen to Malcolm Turnbull writing in *The Guardian* today.[18] He makes the point and he speaks from bitter experience over the Republic of course that having bipartisanship is a necessary but not necessarily a sufficient condition. And with the death of Bill Hayden, I over the weekend was speaking to someone who'd been a Labor minister with Hayden who just very matter of factly said to me because he wasn't involved in this referendum; he said, 'You only try referendums in Australian history in one of two circumstances: either a crisis or where there is absolute consensus.' Now there was never any consensus on this. John Howard in 2007 indicated a willingness that there be something like a preamble or something that Aboriginal leaders would call minimal and symbolic. But he never went with the idea of the voice. Neither did Abbott; neither did Turnbull; neither did Morrison. So there was never bipartisanship. And so I think we can all understand that

Aboriginal Leaders with the publication of this letter are very angry and upset but I think we have to accept that it's simply a given. It doesn't matter what the topic of the referendum. If you do not have bipartisanship there's just no point; and to draw all sorts of other conclusions might not all be altogether warranted.

KG: You mentioned Malcolm Turnbull's piece today. Another thing that he mentioned was the fact that he felt the foundational problem here was that it did go beyond the area where you could get that bipartisanship. You spoke about the symbolic recognition that former prime minister Mr Howard had argued for. Was that the foundational problem here that some of the recommendations, some of the leadership, went too far to get that agreement across the political divide?

FB: It's been the problem all along Kieran because what we've had is the Liberal and National parties have been clear that they're on the table in relation to minimal symbolic change as the Aboriginal leaders would call it. The Aboriginal leaders said they wanted something substantive. Where things started to go wrong in terms of process was in 2012 when Julia Gillard set up her expert panel where they recommended a racial non-discrimination clause. Now that was something substantive. But it could never fly. It was never subjected to the open transparent scrutiny where you get all the lawyers and all the politicians at the table. The same thing happened with this where it was said that yes Aboriginal people gathered at Uluru and they called it a constitutional convention. But there had never been anything like a constitutional convention which was open to the other 97% of Australians. There's been nothing in place since 2017, and so the process was defective from the beginning. And what we then had was after the Garma Festival as you know that there was no move made by the prime minister to set up a process. And by the time there was a parliamentary committee where the Coalition could come to the table it was over: game, set and match. The words were set in concrete. So sadly bipartisanship by means of process was never there, and so it was always doomed.

KG: I do want to get to what's next in a moment because I know you've got some very constructive ideas on what we should do, but just to pick up on something in the Calma/Langton report: it's page 169 — this statement in it that says: 'The national voice should not be able to obstruct or delay government or Parliament. Mechanisms should not create burdensome or bureaucratic compliance processes.' What was in the Calma/Langton report. It seems that the end result was that this proposed amendment went well beyond what had been suggested in that initial analysis by including executive government.

FB: We had a gargantuan leap, Kieran. what was in Calma/Langton, and I was on the Calma/Langton committee, I was there for two years: everyone was on the same page that basically what it was about was a voice to Parliament and to government in relation to laws and policies. But by the words that were adopted at Garma and which were then put forward by government it was not only to include those sorts of things, but also administrative decisions made by a quarter of a million public servants. That was going to set up a whole new bureaucracy that was never envisaged by Calma/Langton. In fact we specified in Calma/Langton that the voice wouldn't even deal with what was called delegated legislation because there were a thousand pieces of such legislation a year. Well, God help us, there'd be a thousand administrative decisions by public servants every week. So it was an enormous overreach and once there was no willingness to tailor it back more consistent with Calma/Langton, then obviously we were in very deep trouble.

KG: And Father Frank, I was interested to read your analysis in the wake of the referendum wipeout in *The Australian* at the weekend where basically you said that constitutional recognition is lost for a generation, and if I can just paraphrase you: you believe governments now need to empower some of the existing bodies including the National Aboriginal Community Controlled Health Organization.

FB: They need to be empowered and listened to now absolutely because what we've got as a situation I think there's goodwill and there's general agreement in the community and on both sides of the political aisle in Canberra that something more has to be done to close the gap, particularly on those ghastly health statistics. Well guess what: we've got a Coalition of Peaks, and there was an agreement which was negotiated with the Morrison government with that Coalition of Peaks about which we've heard next to nothing while the referendum has been playing out. So let's get that Coalition of Peaks working properly. And in terms of health issues, you've got an enormous operation there with NACCHO which represents all the community-based Aboriginal health organizations — all 145 of them. They've got splendid offices there in Constitution Avenue in Canberra. They're headed up by a very competent Aboriginal civil servant, Patricia Turner. And why isn't it that they're not being listened to more closely? I mean during the referendum campaign we had the Minister for Health out there even writing an article saying he needs to listen to a voice but there was no mention of NACCHO or the Coalition of Peaks. So now that the referendum is behind us, I think there's a need for the real work to be done so that NACCHO can be assured that they are right there at the table with the Parliamentary processes and with the minister and that the Coalition of Peaks is now taken seriously even though it was a creation at the time of the Morrison government. Let's get past the party politics and let's start doing something constructive in order to close those gaps.

KG: Yep and Father Frank I know that your view was that some in the debate saw you as a bit of an old fogey with antiquated ideas but unfortunately they didn't listen to you and as the famous saying goes: 'If we don't learn from history, we're doomed to repeat the mistakes'.

FB: We are and I think that what's happened is they played roulette with the country's soul taking us way back. Look at that letter that's come out from the Aboriginal leaders today — the anger, the disappointment, the despair.[19] These are the people we've got to be able to work with well and constructively and in trust in order to close those gaps. And so so much of what Noel Pearson detected as love in the air during the last week or two of the campaign: that's evaporated. Why? Because basically Australians have voted as they've always voted in referendums. They've basically said that we need to be sure that either there is a crisis or that there is consensus among our politicians. And the great tragedy of this, Kieran, is that in the end all you've got to do is listen to people at the family barbecue nowadays. I mean those who blame Albanese are those who are the Tory voters; those who blame Dutton are those who are the Labor voters. And that sort of partisanship should never come into a referendum. Once it does, the referendum is lost completely.

KG: Father Frank Brennan, it's great to get your insights today and right throughout this debate. We'll stay in touch. I appreciate it.

FB: We will, but I fear it'll be another generation before it happens, so probably not in my lifetime Kieran; I hope it's in yours.

The Swag

Summer 2023[20]

At the recent referendum, we priests all knew parishioners and fellow priests who voted 'Yes' with enthusiasm, others who voted 'Yes' with reservations, others who voted 'No' with conviction, and others who voted 'No' with regret. If you were like me, you were happy to recommend that your fellow citizens vote 'Yes' with hope, rather than 'No' with despair.

Some 'Yes' voters thought the proposed change to the Constitution was perfect or at least safe and worthwhile. Others of us thought the wording imperfect but thought the whole thing had dragged on too long – since 2007, and that there was no guarantee that any proposal would be improved in the next 5 or 10 years.

The people spoke loud and clear on 14 October 2023. The referendum was lost in every state and the vote for 'No' was 60% with 'Yes' limping in at 40%. I presume the Catholic vote was much the same.

At the Prime Minister's press conference acknowledging the loss of the referendum on Sunday 15 October, a journalist asked Mr Albanese: 'Why do you think Australians voted No?' He simply answered: 'The analysis will go on for some time, no doubt. But the truth is that no referendum has succeeded in this country without bipartisan support. None.'[21]

There's really not much need for further analysis than that. We all knew that from Day One. And the Prime Minister thought it worth a shot without bipartisan support.

Three months after Mr Albanese made his post-election announcement at the Garma Festival on 31 July 2022 that he would proceed with a referendum this year, two of the respected leaders of the Uluru Dialogues spoke at the National Press Club. One of them, Professor Megan Davis, spoke about the proposed wording announced at Garma and said, 'It's not set in stone, but it's a good beginning.'

When asked about the Opposition Leader's failure to commit at that stage of the process, she said, 'That's in some way the job of an Opposition, to raise these questions. Questions about detail are perfectly legitimate questions.'

Professor Davis insisted that the First Nations leaders of the Uluru dialogues had decided to 'leave the politics for the politicians'. She told the national audience that from their discussions with Opposition members, 'There's strong support from members of the LNP.'[22]

Like many observers that day, I presumed Megan Davis was right. But I was very worried. From my discussions with Opposition members, I knew there was considerable disquiet that the Prime Minister had not set up any process for engagement with them. So I wrote to the Prime Minister making two suggestions:

> Now is the time to set up a parliamentary committee process allowing anyone and everyone to have their 'say' on the proposed words of amendment to place in the Constitution.

> Now is the time to return to formal bipartisan co-operation between the Prime Minister and the Leader of the Opposition so as to maximise the prospect of Coalition support for the referendum.[23]

The government decided it was not time for any of that. They waited another five months before setting up a parliamentary committee. By then the cement had dried. The words of the proposed amendment were set. The formal opposition of both the National and Liberal Parties was set. And voters were starting to turn off the idea of a Voice. They had no idea about what it was, how it would work, and what it would achieve.

Andrew Bragg was a key Liberal Party supporter who served on the parliamentary committee eventually established in April and expected to work on an impossibly short time line. He said: 'The committee process we had was a joke. It did not provide a proper opportunity to improve the wording. I mean, the idea that this wording is perfect, I think, is intellectually insincere.'[24] He told Parliament: 'I think it was a bad process, mainly because there was no effort put into trying to develop a set of words by the parliament. Rather, what was given to the committee was a government bill. We were asked to review a government bill in five weeks, which was a policy of the government.' He said, 'The idea that the way the Voice has been drafted in this bill is perfect is intellectually unsound.'[25] Having appeared before the committee, I agree with Bragg's characterisation of the committee process and outcome. After the referendum, Bragg told the *Sydney Morning Herald*: 'The committee process was a last-chance saloon. That's when the government could have pivoted and tweaked the wording and brought a whole bunch of Liberals across [to Yes]. The government wouldn't compromise on anything. The wording they wanted was the wording they got.'[26]

From there, the referendum was doomed. The first lesson for church leaders and church social justice groups is: don't just sit back and trust government when they depart from the tried and tested processes for constitutional change, when they abuse parliamentary process, and when they ride roughshod over citizens of goodwill wanting to enhance government processes and proposals. The government's novel approach of going it alone with a handpicked group of Aboriginal advisers was never going to work. It was always going to end in disaster. They were playing roulette with the nation's soul. They should have been challenged or at least questioned. The church leadership and church social justice groups were largely silent or implicitly trusting of the government's approach. Don't forget: this was Labor's 25th failed attempt to amend the Australian Constitution. Their one and only success was back in 1946.

The second lesson is that we all have a lot of work to do to educate each other and our fellow citizens about the entitlements of First Australians. We all know parishioners and fellow priests of good will who simplistically assert that all that is required for justice is to treat everyone the same. If that were all that the gospel and Catholic social teaching required, we would of course vote 'No' to any constitutional amendment which accorded a special place to First Australians. We would be readily tempted to think that any special recognition of First Australians would divide the nation.

This problem became manifest 35 years ago when the 14 Australian church leaders sponsored an initiative during 1988, the bicentenary year. They asked that the Australian Parliament pass a resolution in the new Parliament House affirming (a) the importance of Aboriginal and Torres Strait Islander culture and heritage; and (b) the entitlement of Aborigines and Torres Strait Islanders to self-management and self-determination, subject to the Constitution and the laws of the Commonwealth of Australia. The Hawke Labor government was very supportive. At the last minute the Coalition parties in opposition expressed their concern that the entitlement to self-management and self-determination should be qualified by the words 'in common with all other Australians'.[27] This qualification was not acceptable to the church leaders nor to the Aboriginal leaders with whom we were liaising. Thus the motion was passed without the support of the Coalition parties.

Fred Chaney, one of the Liberal Party's most enlightened and passionate advocates for Aboriginal Australians, was leader of his party in the Senate. He told the Senate: 'We, like the Government, have made mistakes but I think one mistake we are not prepared to make is to hand a weapon to people who might use that weapon as a stick to beat a path towards the concept of two nations in this country. The very clear view of the Opposition is that that is a totally counterproductive way to go and the great bulk of Aboriginal people that I have met agree with me.'[28] That's the same sort of thing we heard from the 'No' advocates during the recent referendum campaign. Fred's 1988 words could well be taken up by Senator Jacinta Nampijinpa Price.

For his part, Fred Chaney has developed his thinking these past 35 years and since leaving the Parliament. During the referendum campaign, as a passionate Yes advocate, he wrote: 'The reality is Indigenous Australians, with their unique cultures, are a permanent and distinct part of Australia. The past discredited assimilation policies assumed they would be absorbed and cease to exist in their difference. The old Australia did everything it could to make that happen. Thankfully, it didn't happen. Indigenous people maintained their identities against all the odds that were stacked against them. Now, with even the "No" proponents supporting some form of recognition, and Native Title reminding us and them that Indigenous people already have distinct legal rights, we know that the world's oldest living cultures are here to stay.'[29] Not every member of the Coalition parties has made that change in recent years. I daresay that most 'No' voters, whether or not they be church goers, would be more comfortable with Fred's 1988 declaration rather than his 2023 observations. This is where we have real work to do.

In *Laudato Si'*, Pope Francis wrote: 'it is essential to show special care for indigenous communities and their cultural traditions. They are not merely one minority among others, but should be the principal dialogue partners, especially when large projects affecting their land are proposed.'[30] His predecessor John Paul II at Alice Springs in 1986 said: 'The establishment of a new society for Aboriginal people cannot go forward without just and mutually recognized agreements with regard to (your) human problems, even though their causes lie in the past.'[31] Let's hope that, by the next time we have a referendum on this issue, those in our pews will be convinced that First Australians deserve a special, distinctive place at the table.

Let's be guided by NATSICC who have said, 'With this hope in our hearts, we will continue to advocate for the rights and dignity of Aboriginal and Torres Strait Islander Peoples. We are certain that our family, the Catholic Church continues to walk alongside us. ... We believe that together, with love, understanding, and the grace of God, we can build a future where every individual is recognized, respected, and cherished.'[32]

Homily

29th October 2023[33]

When asked by the Pharisees to name the greatest commandment, Jesus marries love of God and love of neighbour: 'you must love your neighbour as yourself.'

The week started with the publication of the letter by some of the Indigenous leaders of the YES campaign in the failed referendum. They said: 'The truth is that the majority of Australians have committed a shameful act whether knowingly or not, and there is nothing positive to be interpreted from it.'[34] Their anger, pain, and distress are palpable. By week's end, the Prime Minister was trying to put the loss into some historical perspective. Perhaps it was not so much a matter of the people's shame, but the folly of our politicians. Afterall, no referendum has ever succeeded without bipartisan support. Being asked about the loss while in Washington, Mr Albanese explained 'that it is difficult to change the Constitution in Australia. That in order to get people to vote Yes for constitutional change, you have to convince people of all the merits, and in order to get people to vote No, you only need to raise doubt.' He cited the history of other proposals: 'And I have said to people that there are things that have been defeated like payment of just compensation, four-year terms, recognition of local government, in order to try to put it in context — that it is a difficult change.'[35]

Asked to reflect on the referendum loss in my last interview on the matter, I said: 'Look at that letter that's come out from the Aboriginal leaders today — the anger, the disappointment, the despair. These are the people we've got to be able to work with well and constructively and in trust in order to close those gaps. And so much of what Noel Pearson detected as love in the air during the last week or two of the campaign, that's evaporated. Why? Because basically Australians have voted as they've always voted in referendums. They've basically said that we need to be sure that either there is a crisis or that there is consensus among our politicians. And the great tragedy of this is that in the end all you've got to do is listen to people at the family barbecue nowadays. I mean those who blame Albanese are those who are the Tory voters; those who blame Dutton are those who are the Labor voters. And that sort of partisanship should never come into a referendum. Once it does, the referendum is lost completely.'[36]

Unfortunately, the proposed constitutional change was too loosely worded and the process for seeking bipartisanship non-existent. The major challenge for the country in the future is according First Australians agency and self-determination while remaining true to the undoubted rules for constitutional change. We in the church need to get better at calling government to account when they breach such rules or sell short the First Australians of their legitimate entitlements.

There will be ongoing debate about shame and blame. But we need to recommit to that love of neighbour which can herald a new beginning in justice and reconciliation.

A couple of days after the publication of the Aboriginal letter, I was privileged to join a group of 20 people at Australian Catholic University meeting with Katalin Novak, the President of Hungary. The 46 year old mother of three was accompanied by her bishop from the Reformed Church in Hungary. She addressed us and answered questions for well over an hour, and without a note. She is a great advocate for laws and policies aimed at encouraging a higher birth rate in view of Europe's below replacement birth rate. She spoke of the complexity of foreign relations especially with the Ukraine-Russia conflict. Hungary, though dependent on Russian gas during the winter, is sympathetic to the Ukrainians, two million of whom have fled into Hungary during the war. With disarming simplicity and a charming smile, she told us, 'Faith and children help you make the right decisions.' She has a good relationship with Pope Francis with whom she speaks regularly on the phone, and in Spanish. At the end of her presentation, she told us about the moment she took over the presidency two years ago. She was left in an office briefly on her own. So she called her husband. He was too busy to talk. She tried to call her best friend but she was not available. She said, 'But then I realised I was not alone. I always have someone with me.' Her simple profession of faith was inspirational.

The Hungarian president's hopeful message resonated with the note of hope in the despairing letter from the Aboriginal leaders: 'We have faith that the upswelling of support through this referendum has ignited a fire for many to walk with us on our journey towards justice.'

All this is playing out against the backdrop of the appalling situation in Israel and Gaza. None of us has an answer to the escalating violence and killing of innocent non-combatants in this war. The wanton terrorism of Hamas will be avenged and Israel will do all in its power to degrade Hamas as a military and political force in Gaza. But with Hamas being embedded amongst so many innocent Palestinians in confined spaces, civilian casualties will be inevitable.

Political philosopher Michael Walzer has rightly said, 'If terrorists use other people as shields, then anti-terrorists have to find their way around the shields'.[37]

As the conflict continues, the long term and continuing injustices suffered by Palestinians on the West Bank as well as Gaza will fuel resentment of any poorly targeted Israeli interventions. It is now almost 20 years since the International Court of Justice decided by 14-1 that the wall 'and its associated regime gravely infringe a number of rights of Palestinians residing in the territory occupied by Israel, and the infringements resulting from that route cannot be justified by military exigencies or by the requirements of national security or public order.'[38] Even the one dissenting judge, Judge Thomas Buergenthal, accepted that 'the wall is causing deplorable suffering to many Palestinians living in that territory'. He insisted that 'the means used to defend against terrorism must conform to all applicable rules of international law and that a State which is the victim of terrorism may not defend itself against this scourge by resorting to measures international law prohibits.'[39] Back in July 2004, Australia was one of only six countries to dissent from the resolution of the UN General Assembly carried 150-6 with 10 abstentions demanding 'that Israel, the occupying Power, comply with its legal obligations as mentioned in the advisory opinion'.[40]

None of us has the answers to the political, military and moral challenges erupting in the Middle East these days. Praying earnestly for those carrying the heavy responsibility of deciding how to avenge and degrade Hamas while avoiding a conflagration going well beyond the borders of Israel and Gaza, we recall those words of the Lord spoken to Moses in today's first reading from Exodus:

'Tell the sons of Israel this: "You must not molest the stranger or oppress him, for you lived as strangers in the land of Egypt. You must not be harsh with the widow, or with the orphan; if you are harsh with them, they will surely cry out to me, and be sure I shall hear their cry; my anger will flare and I shall kill you with the sword, your own wives will be widows, your own children orphans.'

Contemplating the breakdown in reconciliation here at home and the despair in the Middle East, we can pray together with the Hungarian President Katalin Novak:

I love you, Lord, my strength.

I love you, Lord, my strength,
my rock, my fortress, my saviour.
My God is the rock where I take refuge;
my shield, my mighty help, my stronghold.
The Lord is worthy of all praise,
when I call I am saved from my foes.

I love you, Lord, my strength.

Long life to the Lord, my rock!
Praised be the God who saves me,
He has given great victories to his king
and shown his love for his anointed.

I love you, Lord, my strength.

Eureka Street

8 February 2024[41]

Lessons from the Referendum

It's four months since the referendum. The result was a disaster for the country and a tragedy for First Australians. There has been little appetite for public discussion about lessons to be learnt from this abject failure. Some of the key proponents saw nothing wrong with the process and nothing wrong with the wording of the proposed change. They think that racism played a key part in the result. If they're right, there will be no point in attempting again constitutional recognition of First Australians. But they may be wrong – and I hope they are. There may be a prospect of future constitutional change but not with the process that was adopted and not with the wording that was proposed in 2023. It's time to begin the conversation about past mistakes, before we all start forgetting what went on.

The major challenge for the country in the future will be according First Australians agency and self-determination while remaining true to the undoubted rules for constitutional change. Indigenous leaders will not accept minimal symbolic change to the Constitution. It will be necessary to find that sweet spot of substantive change acceptable to most members of the Commonwealth Parliament. There may be one, but there may not. Finding it will take great trust and collaboration.

The proposed addition of a new chapter of the Constitution setting up the Voice was first suggested by Noel Pearson after it became clear that the recommendation of the 2012 expert panel (of which he was a member) for a racial non-discrimination clause would not fly. Constitutional conservatives had labelled the non-discrimination clause as a one-line bill of rights. It was a thought bubble floated by a hand selected expert panel – a thought bubble which would burst the moment it was subject to scrutiny by a broad range of politicians, lawyers and members of the public.

The idea of a Voice was rejected out of hand over some years by three Liberal prime ministers in a row – Tony Abbott, Malcolm Turnbull and Scott Morrison. The present leader of the opposition, Peter Dutton, was a cabinet minister in all three of those governments, led by prime ministers from all spectrums of the Liberal Party.

Malcolm Turnbull worked in co-operation with Opposition leader Bill Shorten to finalise the membership and mandate of the Referendum Council which authorised the Uluru Dialogues culminating in the Uluru Statement from the Heart published in May 2017. The Referendum Council, like the 2012 expert panel, was a group hand-picked by government. The gathering at Uluru was preceded by a series of community consultations amongst First Nations Peoples. According to Turnbull, prior to those consultations, Noel Pearson informed Turnbull and Shorten back in November 2016 'that he was expecting the Uluru conference to recommend that there be a change to the constitution to establish "a Voice", which would be a national advisory assembly composed of and elected by Aboriginal and Torres Strait Islander peoples.'[42] Shorten had previously said the idea had 'a snowball's hope in hell'. Turnbull agreed, telling Pearson: 'Noel, you can recommend whatever you wish – you're entitled to my honest opinion, not my acquiescence.'[43]

The Uluru Statement from the Heart called for 'the establishment of a First Nations Voice enshrined in the Constitution'. After Uluru, the Referendum Council recommended 'that a referendum be held to provide in the Australian Constitution for a representative body that gives Aboriginal and Torres Strait Islander First Nations a Voice to the Commonwealth Parliament'. This first recommendation made no mention of a Voice to Executive Government. It's important to note that the Referendum Council insisted on separating the Voice from a 'Declaration of recognition'.

The first recommendation did state: 'The body will recognise the status of Aboriginal and Torres Strait Islander peoples as the first peoples of Australia.' But there followed a second recommendation: 'That an extra-constitutional Declaration of Recognition be enacted by legislation passed by all Australian Parliaments, ideally on the same day, to articulate a symbolic statement of recognition to unify Australians.' The Council noted: 'A Declaration of Recognition should be developed, containing inspiring and unifying words articulating Australia's shared history, heritage and aspirations. The Declaration should bring together the three parts of our Australian story: our ancient First Peoples' heritage and culture, our British institutions, and our multicultural unity. It should be legislated by all Australian Parliaments, on the same day, either in the lead up to or on the same day as the referendum establishing the First Peoples' Voice to Parliament, as an expression of national unity and reconciliation.'[44]

This second recommendation fell by the wayside.

A 2018 joint parliamentary committee was set up to consider the way forward; it was chaired by Labor Senator Patrick Dodson and Liberal MP Julian Leeser. Dodson later became the Special Envoy for Reconciliation and the Implementation of the Uluru Statement from the Heart. Leeser was the Shadow Minister for Indigenous Australians until relinquishing the position so he could campaign for the Voice. The committee included Linda Burney and Malarndirri McCarthy who then became the Minister and Assistant Minister for Indigenous Australians respectively. Also on the committee was Warren Snowdon, a long time Labor member of the House of Representatives from the Northern Territory.

The committee was very aware that only eight out of 44 referendums had succeeded since federation. No doubt the Labor members were painfully aware that 24 of Labor's 25 attempts had failed, the only success being the 1946 referendum expanding the Commonwealth's power to grant welfare benefits.

The committee heard from a bevy of constitutional law academics including Professors Anne Twomey, George Williams, Cheryl Saunders, and Megan Davis. They were *ad idem* that a precondition for a successful referendum was some form of elected constitutional convention or sponsored parliamentary process which could include the general public making submissions about any proposed change to the Constitution. Davis agreed with Williams regarding the 'important role that a national convention might play in... enabling non-Indigenous Australians to walk through a deliberative decision-making constitutional process that enables them to better understand the exigency of a Voice to Parliament'[45]. Twomey warned: 'Constitutional commissions or other expert bodies may also be the subject of suspicion because they are invariably appointed by governments. An elected constitutional convention, on the other hand, gives the people a positive role in initiating constitutional reform. On this basis, they [the people] might be more likely to approve, or at least give serious consideration to, the products of its deliberation.'[46]

The committee received 18 very different suggestions for wording to establish a Voice enshrined in the Constitution. For example, Patrick Dodson and Warren Snowdon proposed:

'1. There shall be a First Nations Voice to Parliament;

2. The Voice shall not be a third chamber of the Parliament;

3. The Voice shall be advisory only and its advice will not be justiciable; and

4. Its powers and functions shall be determined by the Parliament of Australia.'[47]

A couple of months after the close off date for submissions, three of the leaders of the Uluru Dialogues (Noel Pearson, Megan Davis and Pat Anderson) submitted a more expansive proposal. The committee was unanimous in the view that 'neither the principle nor the specific wording of provisions to be included in the Constitution are settled. More work needs to be undertaken to build consensus on the principles, purpose and the text of any constitutional amendments.'[48]

The Morrison government did nothing to progress constitutional recognition. But it did establish the Calma/Langton committee to co-design a model for the Voice regardless of whether it be legislated or included in the Constitution. I was privileged to serve on that committee.

The Labor Party in opposition committed itself to full implementation of the Uluru Statement. On election, Prime Minister Anthony Albanese made three captain's picks. First he went to the Garma Festival and announced the Pearson/Davis/Anderson proposal as the preferred model of words for inclusion in the Constitution. He said it could be used 'as the basis for further consultation. Not as a final decision but as the basis for dialogue, something to give the conversation shape and form. I ask all Australians of goodwill to engage on this.'[49]

Second, he abandoned any idea of a constitutional convention or parliament sponsored process for public involvement in the design of the constitutional provision. Instead he handpicked a Referendum Working Group of 21 Aboriginal and Torres Strait Islander persons with whom the government would negotiate in confidence. He thought he could shame Peter Dutton into coming on board without the need for a formal platform including the Opposition.

Third, he appointed an 8-member Constitutional Expert Group including Twomey, Saunders, Williams and Davis, all of whom had previously recommended some form of public cross-party process, but who now were locked into confidential government negotiations with the handpicked group of Aboriginal and Torres Strait Islander representatives.

The proposed constitutional change was too loosely worded and the process for seeking bipartisanship non-existent. For example, the amendment proposed that the Voice could make representations to government on any matters relating to Aboriginal and Torres Strait Islander peoples. This would have included representations being made to public servants prior to the making of routine administrative decisions impacting on Aboriginal and Torres Strait Islander peoples. The proposed wording announced by Prime Minister Albanese at Garma was not the product of a constitutional convention. It was not even the result of a parliamentary process winning support of most members of parliament.

In the absence of agreement about the meaning and scope of tight constitutional wording, the assurances of admirable retired Justices counted for little (like retired Chief Justice Robert French and retired Justice Kenneth Hayne), especially when there was legal disagreement with other reputable, though philosophically other-disposed lawyers (like retired Justice Ian Callinan and the nation's most experienced silk in constitutional litigation, David Jackson). The late Robert Ellicott was Australia's most successful Attorney General steereing through 3 of the 8 successful referendum questions since federation. He was fond of saying 'For a referendum proposal to have a substantial chance of acceptance', it 'should contain no element of possible substantial confusion on legal or other grounds.'[50] Last year we had plenty of substantial confusion with each side quoting their preferred top flight lawyers who could not agree.

During the last sitting week prior to the winter break last year, the government made vain, belated efforts to limit the scope of the new wording proposed for the Constitution, urging us all to read the Attorney General's second reading speech. The contested issue was over the ambit of the clause which provided: 'The Aboriginal and Torres Strait Islander Voice may make representations to the Parliament and the Executive Government of the Commonwealth on matters relating to Aboriginal and Torres Strait Islander peoples.'

Prime Minister Albanese told Parliament that 'the Attorney-General's second reading speech made it very clear that they would advise on "matters specific to Aboriginal and Torres Strait Islander peoples" and, importantly, on "matters ... which affect Aboriginal and Torres Strait Islander peoples differently to other members of the Australian community".'[51]

The Leader of the Opposition, Peter Dutton, told Parliament: 'There are no words that the Attorney-General can include in his second reading speech that will override the words inserted into the Constitution. Let's be very clear about that. The Attorney-General knows that. This legal nonsense that was put forward by the government this week that some sentence inserted by the Attorney-

General into the second reading speech will somehow override the provision in the Constitution is a legal nonsense.'[52]

Dutton was right. Nothing said or done by Parliament could impose limits on the scope of broad language in a proposed constitutional change. Even Kenneth Hayne, one of the government's most preferred retired High Court judges and constitutional advisers, made this clear in the 1998 *Hindmarsh Island Bridge Case*.[53] The Voice would have been able to make representations to Parliament and to all levels of Executive Government (including public servants and agencies such as the Reserve Bank and Centrelink) on any matters relating to Aboriginal and Torres Strait Islander peoples, regardless of whether those matters related to them specifically or differently.

The process for determining the constitutional provision was non-inclusive, and depended on closed door discussions between government and a hand-picked group of Indigenous leaders. The Uluru dialogues excluded not only the National Congress of Australia's First Peoples. It also excluded the Aboriginal members of the Commonwealth Parliament. Attempts to classify Uluru as a constitutional convention were foolish, given that 97% of the Australian voters had no representation whatever at the meeting. There is no point in seeking constitutional change unless there has first been a Constitutional Convention representative of the nation, or else a transparent, inclusive parliamentary process resulting in an all but unanimous recommendation.

It made good sense to include an extensive First Nations consultation process. But it was so structured that those like Warren Mundine and Jacinta Nampijinpa Price were left outside the tent. Lydia Thorpe had been allowed in, but she stormed out. It was folly to presume that the First Nations consultation process could substitute for some style of constitutional convention in which diverse non-Indigenous perspectives could also be at the table.

The idea of the 'Voice' was devoid of content. Some key Indigenous leaders favoured legislation first; others decried any such attempt; while some espoused the tabling of an exposure draft, as occurred with same sex marriage.

The Prime Minister's three major errors were: not seeking any bipartisan approach prior to or immediately after the Garma announcement on 22 July 2022; not providing any detail on the Voice despite the call by those of us on Calma/Langton to legislate first, and despite Noel Pearson's call that an exposure draft bill be produced so that the punters might know what they were voting on (much like same sex marriage); and not setting up any parliamentary supervised process for buy-in by all stakeholders until 4 April 2023. By then the words were set in concrete and voters were hardening in their views. The National Party had already said NO and the Liberal Party was about to do the same. As key Liberal Senator Andrew Bragg said, the parliamentary committee that was then set up was a joke and the drafting of the amendment was intellectually unsound. He'd know because he was on the committee and was a leading Yes supporter from the Liberals.

It was always crazy to think that you could amend the Australian Constitution without a bipartisan process in place, without a fleshed out model of a Voice for voters to understand what they were being asked to vote for, and with a confidential process conducted with a government handpicked group of advisers.

This was nothing like the 1967 referendum or the same sex marriage plebiscite. Those votes were about treating everyone the same. This was asking the Australian people to approve a special provision for Aboriginal and Torres Strait Islander peoples. Many voters of good will wanted to know what it would look like, how it would make a difference, and how it would not divide the country. Too often they were treated as racists or fools.

Previous instances of the Voice – such as ATSIC and the Congress of Australia's First Peoples – were seen to be inadequate, but there was no agreement as to where the 'Voice' would line up on the spectrum of previous instances of a national voice. How would the 'Voice' help close the gap?

There is a need for community groups and leaders to get better at calling government to account when the basic rules of political process are not being followed. Constitutional change is very different from legislative change or a new policy announcement by a government with a fresh electoral mandate.

There is a need for us to better educate people about equality. Equality is not the same as sameness. There is a coherent, developing philosophical tradition about the distinctive rights of Indigenous peoples regardless of their poverty, disadvantage or dispossession. It's time also to confront where there is not common ground in the Australian community. We have absolutely no agreement on the issue of equality under the law. Most of those voters who voted No thought a constitutional voice would divide the nation because the Constitution should treat everyone the same. We Australians are not alone wrestling with this issue of equality. It has three aspects. To what extent should we allow positive discrimination in favour of citizens who together with their ancestors have suffered acute injustice? To what extent should we make special provision for those who rightly claim an Indigenous heritage? To what extent should we recognise perpetual, collective rights rather than individual rights which might be supplemented by temporary special measures to address disadvantage? Though we do not have a bill of rights, we can often learn from the jurisprudence of the US Supreme Court when considering these three questions. While we were engaged in our referendum debate, the US Supreme Court delivered key decisions on equal protection for African-Americans and on the ongoing recognition of the distinctive rights of Native Americans.

There is a need for non-Indigenous Australians to be more attentive to the despair which is being felt by First Australians in the wake of the 40:60 referendum defeat. This is the case especially in those remote communities which voted overwhelmingly in favour of the referendum.

There is a need to educate our fellow Australians about the Constitution and constitutional change. For the average voter, the Australian Constitution is a boring document, little known or understood especially by new Australians and yet it can be amended only by a super-majority of the people. Only 8 of 45 referendums have succeeded. Only 1 of Labor's 26 attempts has succeeded (and that was in 1946). Unless the key elected leaders of the nation are singing from the same hymn sheet, confusion, misunderstanding and mistrust amongst the voting public is inevitable.

There is a need to acknowledge that racism is still an element of Australian society and identity, but racism was NOT a chief cause of the referendum loss. Bipartisanship is a necessary (though not necessarily sufficient) condition for constitutional change. When the process and wording are deficient, more work needs to be done to foster some semblance of bipartisanship.

There is a need to realise that the referendum loss now places the assimilation debate back on the national agenda. Gains of the last generation have been lost. Meanwhile, how do governments and the courts currently address questions of effective and accountable representation of Indigenous interests (in criminal processes, in social welfare agencies, in native title?)

The YES case was conducted on the basis that existing consultative structures between government and First Nations service providers were grossly inadequate. But some of these consultative bodies are well resourced, well respected, and long established. Much of the referendum debate was focused on health needs in remote communities. But we heard little about NACCHO, the National Aboriginal Community Controlled Health Organisation. For example, during the referendum debate, federal Health Minister Mark Butler wrote an opinion piece for *The Australian* on the voice without even mentioning NACCHO or the Coalition of Peaks. He said: 'A voice to the parliament and, frankly, to the health minister, whether they're Labor or Liberal, is a chance to turn a new page in our national efforts to close the gap.'[54] In the absence of a constitutional voice, presumably more could be done to ensure the Coalition of Peaks and NACCHO have a place at the table whenever the Health Minister is considering Indigenous health issues aimed at closing the gap.

Hearing the government ministers during the referendum debate, one could have been forgiven for thinking that the many advisory bodies currently in place did not exist, or that they were not listened to by ministers and senior public servants in Canberra, or that they gave useless advice. Maybe these bodies can be improved. Maybe it's time to audit the performance of the many advisory bodies and better co-ordinate their access to government and to the parliament by means of the parliamentary committee processes.

As I said at the outset of the referendum campaign, the only set of words that had any chance of winning the constitutional double majority was a formula endorsed by both Noel Pearson and John Howard. In his 2022 Boyer Lectures, Pearson said that he had 'engaged with Howard since the 2004 election'[55]. But there is no evidence that the two ever engaged during the referendum campaign other than over the airwaves and with no prospect of agreement. Next time, the leadership will be different, but the same range of unanimity will be required.

Next time we will need an Uluru type process followed by a Constitutional Convention allowing representation of all viewpoints. We should only forego a proper constitutional convention if there is broad support in the Parliament for whatever is recommended by an Uluru type process. The moving image of Pat Anderson, Megan Davis and Noel Pearson at Uluru will need to be supplemented by a similar image of them together with the Prime Minister, the Leader of the Opposition, and the leaders of the minor parties in our Parliament. Without that second frame, forget it. None of us can afford another trainwreck like last year's referendum.

Homily after Lowitja O'Donoghue's Funeral[56]

In today's gospel from John, Jesus says to Nicodemus: 'Whoever lives the truth comes to the light, so that their works may be clearly seen as done in God.' On Friday, I was privileged to attend the State Funeral for Lowitja O'Donoghue – one who lived the truth, one who came into the light, and one whose profound contribution to the nation was seen to be made with a profound and simple faith in Christ. The nation's leaders were there, so too were the Aboriginal leaders who are now household names. Adopting Noel Pearson's phrase, the Prime Minister described her as 'a leader's leader'. He spoke of 'the little girl who longed to be reunited with her mother' who 'somehow transcended the weight of her own experience and grew into a woman of grace, moral clarity and profound inner strength. A woman who grew up in hard country, yet emerged as a figure of such generosity.' Mr Albanese said, 'We celebrate O'Donoghue's life of compassion. Her life of courage. A life in which toughness and tenderness existed in perfect symbiosis.'[57] At the service, Paul Kelly played Lowitja's favourite song, Bob Randall's *Brown Skin Baby*:

> 'My brown skin baby, they take him away
> Between her songs, I heard her say
> Police's been taken my baby away
> From white man, boss, the baby I have
> Why he let him take baby away.'

Lowitja was always a woman of profound Christian faith. She was brought up Baptist but she loved attending St Peter's Anglican Cathedral in Adelaide to hear the old hymns. In 2005, Pope John

Paul II honoured her with a papal award, making her a Dame of the Order of St Gregory the Great. There are not too many Catholics who are papal Dames, let alone Baptists! The state funeral took place in the grand Anglican cathedral in the City of Churches with Bishop Chris McLeod, the Dean of the Cathedral and the National Aboriginal Bishop presiding. Just about every speaker alluded to Lowitja's rock solid Christian faith. Her lifelong friend Pat Anderson recalled Lowitja's deep love for her faith, which gave her joy and 'sustained her in some hard and dark times of which there were many'.

Back in 1997, Lowitja had addressed the National Press Club recalling the passage of the *Native Title Act* in 1993. She said: 'The Native Title Act is a compromise between different and potentially conflicting positions. It represents a carefully constructed balance of interests. It is far from being a caving in to the Indigenous position. Nevertheless, the nation passed a crucial test and reached an historic national settlement. To be at that negotiating table was a very exhilarating experience and I regard the outcome as one of the highlights of my career.'[58]

More recently Paul Keating, who described the native title negotiations as 'the hardest thing I did'[59], said: 'That vast achievement was put in place... by her judgment and good sense in taking up the offer of a conscientious government to invite the Aboriginal nations into a process of justice with the sole aim of dealing with the principal Indigenous grievance – the wilful expropriation of their lands.'[60]

Back in 1993, all was not plain sailing. On Black Friday, 8 October 1993, negotiations had broken down and Keating had let fly as only Keating could. He said, 'I am not sure whether Indigenous leaders can ever psychologically make a change to decide to come into a process, be part of it, and take the burdens of responsibility which go with it.' Delivering the Lowitja Oration in 2011, he said that he was not sure 'whether they could ever summon the authority of their own community to negotiate for and on their behalf'. Looking back, he said:

> 'I like to think those remarks helped galvanise Lowitja O'Donoghue's view as to what needed to be done. But as it turned out – only she could do it. She was the chair of ATSIC. This gave her a pulpit to speak from but no overarching authority, much less power. But this is where leadership matters: she decided, alone decided, that the Aboriginal and Torres Strait Islander peoples of Australia would negotiate, and I emphasise negotiate, with the Commonwealth government of Australia – and that the negotiators would be the leaders of the Indigenous land councils. She decided that. And from that moment, for the first time in the 204-year history of the settled country, its Indigenous people sat in full concert with the government of it all.'[61]

Between Black Friday and Ruby Tuesday ten days later when the native title deal was struck, Lowitja worked tirelessly to bring everyone to the table of principled compromise. Through all these complexities and intrigues, Lowitja held a steady course with an unerring instinct about where to find true north.

On Friday, everyone in the cathedral was painfully aware of the result of last year's referendum which was a disaster for the country and a tragic loss for First Australians. Pat Anderson who was instrumental in the Uluru Dialogues leading up to the referendum reminded the congregation of Lowitja's words in 1997: 'We cannot lose the will to resolve these issues, because they will not go away. But tackling them half-heartedly or high-handedly will be a recipe for continuing failure. I believe that solutions are at hand. But they will require determination and patient effort, negotiation and compromise, imagination and true generosity.'[62]

Pat stressed the need for principled compromise. She also observed: 'In the fierce policy and political battles that went with the job, Lowitja was remarkable in that she never held a grudge. She never held a grudge, she was always willing to work with other people.'

Lowitja O'Donoghue served her people with high dedication and unremitting faith, never bearing a grudge, always willing to forgive, and constantly being committed to principled compromise. The Prime Minister recalled her address to the UN General Assembly in 1992 when she told the community of nations: 'We have become marginalised in our own country'. As Mr Albanese put it: 'Yet, showing the mutually reinforcing strength and grace that were such defining features of her character, O'Donoghue spoke of celebrating her people's survival. A celebration that entailed looking "with hope to our future". As she put it: "We do not wish to conquer or oppress. Nor indeed do we wish to retaliate for two centuries of injustice. Rather we seek to create a new partnership based upon understanding, co-operation and goodwill. The past cannot be changed; our future is in our hands."'

We all gave thanks for the life of one who, as Pat Anderson put it, 'never stopped campaigning for justice for us. She did this with characteristic toughness, humour and grace'. With gusto we all sang the old favourites: *The Old Rugged Cross*, and *We Shall Overcome*.

In today's first reading from the *Book of Chronicles*, we hear of the suffering and dispossession of the Chosen People. Liberation comes to hand when Cyrus, King of Persia, proclaims:

'All the kingdoms of the earth the Lord, the God of heaven, has given to me, and he has also charged me to build him a house in Jerusalem, which is in Judah. Whoever, therefore, among you belongs to any part of his people, let him go up, and may his God be with him!'

Inspired by the profound Christian life and leadership of Lowitja O'Donoghue, we console ourselves with the assurance given to Nicodemus: 'Whoever lives the truth comes to the light, so that their works may be clearly seen as done in God.' Mr Albanese described Lowitja as 'as one of the great rocks around which the river of our history has gently bent, persuaded to flow along a better course'. Inspired by the old hymns as well as the old favourites like *The Old Rugged Cross* and *We Shall Overcome*, we commit ourselves to playing our small part in shaping a river course kindly to all and we pray:

By the streams of Babylon
    we sat and wept
    when we remembered Zion.
On the aspens of that land
    we hung up our harps.

For there our captors asked of us
    the lyrics of our songs,
And our despoilers urged us to be joyous:
    "Sing for us the songs of Zion!"

How could we sing a song of the LORD
    in a foreign land?
If I forget you, Jerusalem,
    may my right hand be forgotten!

May my tongue cleave to my palate
    if I remember you not,
If I place not Jerusalem
    ahead of my joy.

2

My Formal Representations to Government and Parliament

Letter to Prime Minister Albanese, 9 November 2022

Dear Mr Albanese

Thank you for your commitment to holding a referendum on 'the Voice' in the next financial year, during the first term of your government.

Today, like many Australians, I heard Professor Megan Davis and Pat Anderson AO speak at the National Press Club.

Professor Davis made a number of points which now require close attention.

Speaking of your proposed wording for the constitutional change which you announced at the Garma Festival on 30 July 2022, she said, 'It's not set in stone, but it's a good beginning.'

When asked about the Opposition Leader's failure to commit at this stage of the process, she said, 'That's in some way the job of an Opposition, to raise these questions. Questions about detail are perfectly legitimate questions.'

Professor Davis insisted that the First Nations leaders of the Uluru dialogues had decided to 'leave the politics for the politicians'. She told the national audience that from their discussions with Opposition members, 'There's strong support from members of the LNP.'

As a non-Indigenous Australian with a longtime commitment to constitutional recognition, could I put two suggestions:

> **Now is the time to set up a parliamentary committee process allowing anyone and everyone to have their 'say' on the proposed words of amendment to place in the Constitution.**

Even if the parliamentary committee were to conclude that your Garma formula was the appropriate formula, this would be a worthwhile and necessary exercise as it would transform the formula from (a) the government's suggestion in consultation with First Nations leaders and their advisers, to (b) the parliament's proposal to be put to the Australian people.

Such a process would also allow heightened scrutiny of any proposed wording, minimising the risk of unintended consequences.

Such a process would enhance the prospect of buy-in and ownership by the Federal Opposition and all other parties in the Parliament. You will recall that Noel Pearson in his first Boyer Lecture referred to your Garma proposal and then said, 'We know the nation's leader must be joined by all his counterparties in the federal parliament'. If not now, when?

> **Now is the time to return to formal bipartisan co-operation between the Prime Minister and the Leader of the Opposition so as to maximise the prospect of Coalition support for the referendum.**

You will recall that on 17 September 2014 Prime Minister Tony Abbott and Leader of the Opposition Bill Shorten met to discuss constitutional recognition after which Mr Shorten said, 'It needs to be bipartisan, it needs to be meaningful, and it needs to be something which all Australians can get behind and say, "At last, we are going to let our constitution catch up to the world we live in."'

Then on 19 March 2015, Mr Abbott agreed to convene a meeting with Mr Shorten and key indigenous leaders. That meeting then took place at Kirribilli House on 5 July 2015. They jointly agreed to a way forward.

The Referendum Council was then jointly appointed by the new Prime Minister Malcolm Turnbull and Bill Shorten on 7 December 2015. On 20 October 2016, Messrs Turnbull and Shorten then approved the way forward for the Referendum Council to proceed.

Then on 25 November 2016 Messrs Turnbull and Shorten met with the four Aboriginal members of parliament (Labor members Patrick Dodson, Linda Burney and Malarndirri McCarthy and Liberal member Ken Wyatt), and Noel Pearson after a meeting of the Referendum Council when Mr Pearson 'said that he was expecting the Uluru conference to recommend that there be a change to the Constitution to establish "a Voice", which would be a national advisory assembly composed of and elected by Aboriginal and Torres Strait Islander peoples.'

After community consultations and the publication of the Uluru Statement from the Heart, Messrs Turnbull and Shorten announced on 1 March 2018 their agreement on the scope of a new parliamentary committee that would seek to find common ground and work towards a successful referendum on Indigenous recognition in the Constitution.

Your predecessors as Prime Minister and as Leader of the Opposition displayed a level of bipartisanship on process for advancing this matter – a level not usual in other matters of public policy. It is needed once again if there is to be any prospect of deciding a formula of words for insertion into the Constitution which is acceptable to the key First Nations leaders, the Government and the Opposition. Without the support of all three, you know that there is no realistic prospect of 'the Voice' being inserted in the Constitution.

I wish you well in this exercise of national statesmanship. It is now 15 years since Prime Minister John Howard placed constitutional recognition on the national agenda. For the good of our First Nations peoples, for the good of public administration and for the good of the nation, it is essential that this matter now be brought to timely successful resolution. In my humble opinion, that cannot be done without your government now taking the prompt initiative to call the Opposition to the table.

Letter to Prime Minister Albanese
and Leader of the Opposition Dutton
5 March 2023

The Hon Anthony Albanese MP
Prime Minister
Parliament House Canberra
ACT 2600

The Hon Peter Dutton MP
Leader of the Opposition Parliament House
Canberra
ACT 2600

Dear Prime Minister and Leader of the Opposition

Following the exchange of letters between you on 7 January 2023 and 1 February 2023, there was the Prime Minister's statement on 1 March 2023: 'I've said I'll consider anything that's put forward in good faith. What I don't see from the Opposition, or from the leadership of the Opposition anyway, is good faith at the moment. There aren't suggestions coming forward. There is a conscious decision to try to confuse the issue.' This does not bode well for the process and timing of the proposed referendum in October-November 2023.

I understand there will be no parliamentary committee in place until the end of this month and the government presently intends to introduce a bill at that time containing a proposed formula of words to be put at referendum to amend the Australian Constitution.

I am an Australian citizen with a strong commitment to Indigenous recognition in the Constitution through the placement of a Voice in the Constitution. I have serious reservations about the Garma formula of words, especially with provision for the Voice to have a constitutional entitlement to make representations to Executive Government, including all Commonwealth public servants making administrative decisions which may affect any Aboriginal or Torres Strait Islander person.

I am worried that a 'yes' vote might not carry because of the deficiencies in the process for general community consultation and input, and because the proposed formula of words will be too broad risking the clogging of the workings of government and ongoing litigation in the High Court.

So I would like to take this opportunity to give advance notice of the proposals I will be putting to the parliamentary committee for consideration as words of amendment to be put to the people at referendum. I do so, simply so that you might have additional time for consultation with members of your own parties and for the obtaining of competent legal advice.

I make no pretence that my suggestions would be deserving of carriage. But I suspect from my own discussions with a range of citizens that there will be many similar suggestions being put. It is unreal to expect that the Australian public will be satisfied with a six week process for consultation and determination. Let's remember that Aboriginal and Torres Strait Islander representatives will have been afforded eight months for their input to the proposed amendment to the Constitution.

The tragedy I am wanting to avoid is a 'No' vote carried because of flaws in the process resulting in a lack of time for real community engagement and for proper legal analysis.

Be assured my willingness to discuss these proposals with you or your officers, even before the institution of the committee process.

My suggestions are attached.

Wishing you well in your deliberations on this matter which is critical to our national life at this time.

Attachment:

Suggested amendments to the Constitution

1. Insert prior to Chapter 1:

Chapter 1A

The Aboriginal and Torres Strait Islander Peoples

1A. The people of the Commonwealth:

> 1. recognise that the continent and the islands now known as Australia were first occupied by Aboriginal and Torres Strait Islander peoples.

> 2. acknowledge the continuing relationship of Aboriginal and Torres Strait Islander peoples with their traditional lands and waters.

> 3. acknowledge and respect the continuing cultures,

languages and heritage of Aboriginal and Torres Strait Islander peoples.

1B. In recognition of Aboriginal and Torres Strait Islander peoples as the First Peoples of Australia, there shall be an Aboriginal and Torres Strait Islander Voice with such structure and functions as the Parliament deems necessary to facilitate consultation prior to the making of special laws with respect to Aboriginal and Torres Strait Islander peoples, and with such other functions as the Parliament determines.

2. Delete s.25.

3. Amend s.51(xxvi) to read:

Aboriginal and Torres Strait Islander peoples for whom it is deemed necessary to make special laws;

Should these three amendments be unacceptable, I would suggest:

Insert s.127:

In recognition of Aboriginal and Torres Strait Islander peoples as the First Peoples of Australia, there shall be an Aboriginal and Torres Strait Islander Voice with such structure and functions as the Parliament deems necessary to facilitate consultation prior to the making of special laws with respect to Aboriginal and Torres Strait Islander peoples, and with such other functions as the Parliament determines.

Note to Ministers

22 March 2023[63]

The recent remarks of Robert French and Bret Walker are helpful in identifying the real problem with the Voice having a constitutional entitlement to make representations not just to Parliament and ministers but also to public servants.

French has said: 'The proposed amendment to paragraph three, allowing the parliament to make laws about the legal effect of representations, may reduce the risk of an implication that the executive would be legally bound to take them into account.' (See article in *The Australian:* 'Benefits of Indigenous voice to parliament far outweigh risks'.[64])

My concern has not been so much with the legal effect of representations, but rather with the (arguable) constitutional requirement that public servants (a) give notice of an intention to make an administrative decision on a matter relating to any Aboriginal or Torres Strait Islander person; and (b) entertain any representation then received from the Voice before making such a decision.

It is one thing to renew public administration in this way through legislative change which would permit future adjustment. It is another thing to constitutionalise such a renewal rendering the mode of relating between the Voice and the Commonwealth bureaucracy a matter of High Court jurisprudence rather than parliamentary oversight.

Walker has told *The Australian Financial Review* that he does see one scenario for litigation: 'If the Voice was muffled or muted to the point of silence. Of course that would go to court, and probably in the form of mandamus [a judicial writ] against whomever has refused, say, to receive messages from the Voice. It wouldn't be litigation compelling anyone to agree with the latest message of the Voice. Nonsense. That will never happen.' (See article in the *Australian Financial Review:* 'Why Bret Walker says Voice litigation won't matter.'[65])

And this is the issue. The Voice will know what Parliament is up to, and thus will be able to make representations. But if the Voice is kept in the dark about what thousands of public servants are up to in making administrative decisions impacting Aboriginal and Torres Strait Islander persons every day, then of course the Voice will be able rightly to claim that they have been 'muffled or muted to the point of silence'. No one is seriously suggesting that it would be good enough just to leave it to the Voice to discover if a public servant was about to make a decision, and that the Voice's ignorance of same would be a matter of supreme indifference to the courts.

As Walker says: 'Of course that would go to court, and probably in the form of mandamus [a judicial writ] against whomever has refused, say, to receive messages from the Voice.' And one might add: whomever has failed to inform the Voice that they are considering making a decision, and whomever has failed to give the Voice sufficient information about the proposed decision so that the Voice might make a sensible representation.

Walker is surely right when he says: 'It wouldn't be litigation compelling anyone to agree with the latest message of the Voice. Nonsense. That will never happen.' But it might be litigation compelling the public servant to give due consideration to the latest message of the Voice. And it is a brave counsel who would suggest that the parameters of that due consideration can be set down confidently in advance even if the Voice's novel mandate be only statutory. What then if it is a sacred constitutional mandate?

French has addressed a side issue and Walker has nailed the problem but without adverting to the scope of the problem.

Representations to Parliament considering new laws are one thing. Representations to ministers considering policies or practices, another. Representations to public servants making routine administrative decisions are an altogether different matter. Why is it unreal to envisage in future a barrage of applications to the Federal Court, Federal Circuit Court and AAT on a scale similar to that of asylum claims. It's not good enough to be told, 'The Voice wouldn't be interested in doing that.' If they would never be so interested, why give the Voice that constitutional entitlement in the first place?

I have no objection in principle to the Voice having a statutory entitlement to make representations to public servants on administrative decisions relating to Aboriginal and Torres Strait Islander persons. Such a wide sweeping administrative law reform would be subject to legislative amendment should there be any unforeseen consequences or inordinate cost burdens bearing little substantive change to the quality of administrative decision making. But the creation of a one-line constitutional entitlement is the equivalent of the 2012 expert panel's suggestion that the *Racial Discrimination Act 1975* be replaced by a one line constitutional prohibition on discrimination.

I was heartened to read Minister Burney's response at the press conference on 17 March 2023 when she was asked: 'You anticipate a voice be given the powers to advise parliament and government or just parliament?'

She replied: 'The decisions around that will be finalised in the next week or two. But the Uluru Statement was very clear and it was a Voice to advise the Parliament. So take that in its broadest sense. Of course, the principles that have been determined about the Voice stand, including its accountability, including its inclusivity, which is extraordinarily important. Importantly, there will be gender parity. Those things are extremely important. There has been some very good work done around expanding those principles. I'm not going to get ahead of either the Engagement Group, the Working Group or the cabinet on final decisions.' (see transcript: Media Conference – Referendum Working Group & Engagement Group, Adelaide.[66])

So presumably the Garma formula including Parliament and Executive Government no longer stands, or as intimated, will not pass muster with the Cabinet. My major concern about the original Garma formula stems from the fact that under the Constitution, Executive government includes ministers and 'other officers', namely public servants (s.67).

If Cabinet is wanting to maintain as much as possible of the Garma formula (together with the Solicitor General's recommended addition), could I suggest you consider using language as found in s.64 of the Constitution and provide:

In recognition of Aboriginal and Torres Strait Islander peoples as the First Peoples of Australia:

> **1. There shall be a body, to be called the Aboriginal and Torres Strait Islander Voice.**

2. **The Aboriginal and Torres Strait Islander Voice may make representations to Parliament and** *to the Queen's Ministers of State for the Commonwealth* **on matters relating to Aboriginal and Torres Strait Islander Peoples.**

3. **The Parliament shall, subject to this Constitution, have power to make laws with respect to the composition, functions, powers and procedures of the Aboriginal and Torres Strait Islander Voice and the legal effect of its representations.**

If there is a desire by Cabinet to include representations to Commonwealth officers other than ministers, could I respectfully urge that advice first be sought from the Department of Social Services, the Department of Health and Aged Care, the Department of Employment and Workplace Relations, the Department of Education and the Department of Prime Minister and Cabinet.

A comprehensive constitutional change to the system of public administration should be proposed to the Australian people only once competent advice has been provided to the Cabinet.

Of late, there has been much praise of the South Australian Voice. Let's remember that it is only a creation of statute. The national Voice is to be marked by three constitutional characteristics:

1. A form of constitutional recognition of Aboriginal and Torres Strait Islander peoples

2. A constitutional hook for a constitutional entity having a strictly defined constitutional entitlement to make representations to Parliament and perhaps to Ministers

3. A constitutional hook on which can then be hung a vast range of statutory functions amendable by Parliament, including, if desired, a statutory entitlement to make representations to

public servants prior to the making of routine administrative decisions relating to Aboriginal and Torres Strait Islander persons.

The Prime Minister this week has confirmed the need for right process and the right wording in order to attract bipartisan support. It is heartening to see the constructive contribution made in the Senate debate on the *Referendum (Machinery Provisions) Amendment Bill* 2022 by Senators Andrew Bragg and Dean Smith. Given their experience in the same sex marriage plebiscite, it is imperative that the government and the Indigenous Working Group settle on a formula of words acceptable to them and to the Shadow Minister Julian Leeser who has been co-operative throughout this whole process despite the unavailability to date of any parliamentary forum for formal input on the proposed wording of the constitutional amendment. A referendum fought with those three advocating 'No' would be a disaster for everyone.

I would still recommend a provision along these lines:

s.127: In recognition of Aboriginal and Torres Strait Islander peoples as the First Peoples of Australia, there shall be an Aboriginal and Torres Strait Islander Voice with such structure and functions as the Parliament deems necessary to facilitate consultation prior to the making of special laws with respect to Aboriginal and Torres Strait Islander peoples, and with such other functions as the Parliament determines.

As ever, happy to discuss with you or any member of your staff at any time.

Evidence to Parliamentary Committee

1 May 2023[67]

BRENNAN, Father Frank, Private capacity

CHAIR: Thank you, Father Brennan, for appearing before the committee today. There is an opportunity for you to give a short opening statement if you wish. We have the benefit of your submissions, and I think many people have read your opinion that was published today. If you want to table part of your opening submission, that would be appropriate as well. But I'll give you an opportunity to make a very short opening statement.

Father Brennan: Thank you. I'm very grateful for the opportunity to address the committee and answer your questions. I've been a long-time advocate of constitutional recognition of Indigenous Australians. I first wrote a book, *Sharing the Country*, in 1991. In recent years, I wrote *No Small Change* and then the book *An Indigenous Voice to Parliament: Considering a constitutional bridge*. A revised edition of that has just come out this week, and I'd like to present both of those to the committee.

As a non-Indigenous Australian with a strong commitment to Indigenous recognition, I've seen my role as trying to maximise the prospect of the country getting to 'yes'. I'm not a natural optimist on these things, and I know something of the constitutional history. I have made—I will admit—some failed attempts over the last year or so to try and get some bipartisan approaches on this issue. As a country we are in a very difficult position at the moment. But, in terms of trying to get to 'yes', it's essential to address the situation that, politically, getting there as a country without the major parties onboard is a very difficult task. Things have become very partisan indeed.

Therefore, what is necessary is to get the formula of words for proposal to the Constitution as good as possible, with the hope, if I might say, that it might attract onboard some of the key Liberals, like Senator Bragg, a member of this committee, and also people like the member for Berowra. Thus, I think it is important to try and address that question. From my point of view, constitutional recognition has been essential. Since the Uluru statement, what has been non-negotiable is that there be an Indigenous voice recognised in the Constitution. The question then is how that is best to be done. It's to that that I've dedicated my efforts, and I'm more than happy to take your questions.

CHAIR: Thank you very much. I'm going to start with the deputy chair, who I understand has questions for you.

Mr WOLAHAN: Thank you, Father Brennan. What is your proposed amendment to section 129 as drafted, and what is the problem that your amendment is attempting to solve?

Father Brennan: My proposed amendment is very simple. It's that the words 'executive government' be replaced with the words 'ministers of state'. I might just give a brief explanation of that. You've heard from far more learned lawyers than me on this, and you've heard all sorts of disagreements. I think there's furious agreement that parliament should control the way in which representations are received from the Voice, both to parliament and to executive government. The one critical question is the extent to which you constitutionalise that in clause (ii).

So let's look at the sorts of things that the Voice would be looking at. I'm taking as something of a model the much-lauded South Australian model, which has now been announced—namely a voice which will address parliament, a voice which will be in a position to meet with the cabinet and a voice which will meet with the permanent heads of government departments. There's no idea that they'll spend their time down in the weeds meeting with lots of public servants, particularly in relation to administrative decisions. As I've heard Indigenous Australians speaking, what they want is a voice which can be eloquent, loud and taken seriously when it comes to parliament and executive government considering matters of law, policy, practices and procedures.

The one issue which I find difficult is this: the words, as they are at the moment, extend to executive government including public servants making routine administrative decisions. With a quarter of a million Commonwealth public servants, how do you deal with that in terms of it being constitutionalised? We've heard from all the legal experts that, under clause (iii), parliament can do what it likes, except for this: parliament cannot extinguish the capacity that's there under clause (ii). If, under clause (ii), executive government has a capacity to make representations to individual public servants about administrative decisions, then legitimate questions arise, such as: how is the Voice to know that an individual public servant is making an administrative decision which could affect Aboriginal and Torres Strait Islander people? For the Voice to make an adequate representation, how are they to have enough information available to be able to make a coherent representation? All my amendment is aimed at is saying that I agree with all of those legal experts who have said: 'Legislate all you like for the Voice to be not only a voice to parliament and not only a voice to ministers on matters of policy and practices. If you like, legislate for the Voice to be able to make representations to individual public servants on routine administrative decisions.' But that's got to be done by legislation, and to constitutionalise it is to risk that, in the future, as ex-justices Hayne and French have said, if you were to draw the implication that they were to have information about what could be done, that could clog the system of government. I think my simple amendment does achieve that purpose.

Mr WOLAHAN: Thank you. I assume you've read the Solicitor-General's opinion.

Father Brennan: I have.

Mr WOLAHAN: Did that opinion give you comfort that the risk that you identify is not a problem to worry about?

Father Brennan: It gave me comfort about matters to do with avoiding clogging of the system once a representation has been received. It gave me no comfort whatever in terms of the question about how the Voice would ever be apprised of the matter when a public servant was making a decision. How would the Voice ever be apprised of sufficient information in order to be able to make a coherent representation? You'll be aware that question (2) put to the Solicitor-General—on page 5—was specifically asking about the power of the parliament to determine matters after a representation has been received. There's no comfort to be found in terms of what complexity there might be before a representation is made. I'm just going on, if I may say, the ordinary Australian instinct for 'the fair go'. If a constitutional protection came down saying to the Voice:

'If you happen to know a public servant is making a decision about something, then you can go and make a representation. But there's no need for that public servant to tell you anything about what they're considering to do.' In fairness, you'd want to say: 'If there's a capacity to make those representations, it should be in relation to decisions generally.' I think that requires a very complex statutory scheme. I don't think it can be done just with a simple one-line entry in the Constitution in clause (ii).

Mr WOLAHAN: Highly credentialled and qualified legal experts have given evidence of their assessment of the risk and have differing views on how to quantify it. Do you agree that, based on the evidence we have heard, it would still be reasonably open for a future High Court to find a risk of an implied duty to consult or consider?

Father Brennan: It's a brave mere mortal who comes before you and says: 'Yes, you've got French and Hayne on the one hand and Callinan on the other, so what's it to be?' I don't know what it's going to be. If you all know what it's going to be, then good luck to you. What I do know is that if you constitutionalise something—including the constitutional entitlement of a constitutional entity, which is to be a very sacred entity in the life of the nation—to have an entitlement to make representations to public servants, then I think over time there will be implications drawn. I am aware at the moment that French and Hayne say: 'Oh no, we'd never draw any implications, because if we did we know it would basically stuff up the system of government.'

If I might draw a parallel, and quote people far more expert than myself in academia, you've got submission 92 there by Professors Aroney and Gerangelos, who have written one of the key texts in academe on the Australian Constitution. They point out at paragraph

25 that, for example, the Constitution presently states that members of the House of Representatives and senators—yourselves—will be 'directly chosen by the people'. Looking at those words, you'd say: 'You wouldn't draw any implications out of any of that, would you?' It took some years, but for the High Court—ultimately in the Lange case—as Aroney and Gerangelos point out. They said that the High Court has implied that if they're directly chosen by the people, then the people have to have an opportunity to gain an appreciation of the available alternatives. Therefore, we pare back the law of defamation and we enhance the capacity for freedom of speech. I would say, equally, that if you maintain a constitutional entitlement to make representations to public servants not just about developing policy or whatever but about routine administrative decisions, over time there's all the scope for drawing what is only a sensible implication.

If I could put it this way, you heard very eloquently and very directly from people like Professor Williams and Bret Walker, who are far more learned in the law than me, they at least conceded that you couldn't have a public servant just putting plugs in the ears and saying: 'I won't receive your representation.' The only sort of implication I'm talking about is what if the public service says: 'We're not going to block our ears. We're just going to lock the building. We're just not going to let you in. We're not going to let the Voice know what are the routine administrative decisions being made by public servants.' Everyone agrees that that can be done under legislation under clause (iii), provided it doesn't squash clause (ii). That's why I say amend clause (ii) to 'parliament and ministers of state'.

The Voice, like the South Australian Voice, wants to be eloquent. It doesn't want to be getting down in the weeds with public servants. It wants to be a voice which is eloquent to parliament and to the ministers. As one ex-minister said to me: 'If you want to get public servants doing the right thing in this sort of area, don't go to them. Go to the minister. Get the minister to correct the public servants and draw them into line.' That's what my amendment is directed at.

Mr WOLAHAN: Thank you, and my final question is: in turning our minds to that future High Court—and it may be a long time in the future—in their deliberation on the risk of a duty to consult or consider, because there is furious agreement that this would be unworkable and some say catastrophic for the workings of government, should we as a parliament in drafting the words not reduce that risk as much as we can?

Father Brennan: I would have thought so, particularly when you've got before you a choice. You can stay with the present words where there is that risk, or you can amend those words to 'ministers of state' where you eliminate that risk. You can still have parliament giving that entitlement to the Voice if they want to under clause (iii). They can make all the representations they like to individual public servants making routine administrative decisions but avoiding the prospect of that risk. I can do no better than quote the elegance of Bret Walker to you where he said:

I would just add this:

he said this at page 48 of his evidence—

subsection (iii) is not allowed to eat subsection (ii). That's what it means, to say that it's subject to the Constitution. So you can't, under subsection (iii), by what I'll call pretended regulation of functions, effectively, substantially, really deprive the Voice of its definitional character, which is one of making representations.

If you constitutionalise the entitlement to make representations to public servants about routine administrative decisions under clause (ii), you cannot allow clause (iii) to eat clause (ii). So, in terms of getting something which is workable and which reduces those risks—and I say why I think this is a slam dunk—is if that amendment was made—and I readily concede it's not for me to make it, it's probably not for you to make it, but I would urge people who are in a position to make these decisions—if that change was made, you can still maintain all the political capacity for the Voice to make representations to public servants about routine matters if that's what you as the parliament want, but you just wouldn't do it constitutionalising under clause (ii). You would eliminate that risk. And a future High Court, make no mistake, would look at the fact and say: 'Well, hang on, parliament could have decided to use the words "ministers of state" but parliament has deliberately used the words "executive government". Parliament intended that it be extended to be making representations to public servants on routine administrative decisions, and we as the High Court of Australia will solemnly commit ourselves to that.' And, yes, pace Justices French and Hayne, they won't be there in 40 years time, like the High Court in Lange coming to interpret the provision about how you elect senators et cetera. The High Court could well say, 'Well, if you're going to make representations to public servants, then of course it's a common courtesy to use the Prime Minister's words, common decency to the Voice to let them know what the public servants are doing and to give them enough information so they can make an intelligent intervention.

Mr WOLAHAN: Thank you, Father Brennan.

Senator WHITE: Can I clarify: in principle, you do support enshrining an Aboriginal and Torres Strait Islander Voice in the Constitution, don't you?

Father Brennan: Absolutely, and have ever since the Uluru Statement was issued. If I might, perhaps immodestly, remind you that none other than Lowitja O'Donoghue invited me to give the Lowitja Oration on the 50th anniversary of 1967 referendum within a fortnight of the Uluru Statement, and I made it abundantly clear. I readily admit I said I thought it should be legislated first so the public could understand it, and I readily admit that we should work for a bipartisan approach. But, in terms of a commitment to a Voice in the Constitution, unequivocally yes.

Senator WHITE: If we don't make the amendments that you suggest, are you going to be voting for it yourself?

Father Brennan: I imagine I would be voting for it, but, with respect, that's not the critical issue. I'm giving a lot of talks around the country on this at the moment. I've been talking in Darwin and Brisbane and zooming into Mount Isa in recent days, and I can assure you there are three groups in the Australian community: there are those who will vote 'yes' no matter what you will say, there are those who will vote 'no' no matter what you say and there are those in the middle who want information, and some of those who want information want to be sure that what is there is legally watertight. It's to those people that I am investing so much of my energy, but in answer to your question: yes.

Senator WHITE: I understand that, but I'm just trying to get it clear because for some people the nuances of making an opinion on legally how it might go versus what you're going to do as a private individual get mixed. And I want it to be clear that you have been an extremely long-term campaigner, very committed to this constitutional recognition. And you're giving this view to us based on what your legal view is, but you also see that the idea of having the Voice or having constitutional recognition is extremely important. That's the nuance of the position and that's why I asked the question. So I do think it is relevant.

Father Brennan: Could I simply add, though, with respect, that we are at the stage of the legislative process at the moment. How one's going to vote on the final outcome—yes, it's an interesting political question, but at this stage of the legislative process this is the one opportunity which is afforded the Australian public to participate with you in saying, 'Let's try and get the wording as right as we can so that we can really get the country to "yes", and not just get over the line but do it in a way which attracts mass support.'

Senator WHITE: I understand where you're coming from, and it's from a position of not trying to scuttle it but to try and make it the best that you can. But the evidence that we have seen is that there have been differing opinions on this matter. And you're in a minority; there's no doubt about it. We've seen very, very different opinions from the Solicitor-General, former High Court justice Kenneth Hayne, former chief justice Robert French, Professor George Williams, Professor Anne Twomey, Professor Asmi Wood, Professor Cheryl Saunders, Bret Walker SC, Arthur Moses SC, Matthew Howard SC, Professor Gabrielle Appleby, the New South Wales Bar Association, the Law Council of Australia and a whole lot of others that I won't name.

We've got to decide, when we hear legal opinions, how we weigh them all up and what we recommend in our report. That's our job. That doesn't mean a minority person could not be right, but when you've got an avalanche of opinion against you—it is something that we have to weigh up. So in making your legal opinion, why—I struggle with what you're saying. Part of it is that you think you'll get more people into voting yes. Is that right? Because if you reduce the consultation mechanism, you say, more people will vote yes. Is that the essence of what you are saying? Or are you saying it's open to challenge? What is it, succinctly?

Father Brennan: You've put a political question to me. There are three reasons. Firstly, yes, as I've said quite brazenly, I would hope that such an amendment could bring on board some Liberals like Senator Bragg, on your committee, and the member for Berowra. Secondly, I would hope it would help to bring on board more members of the public who are agnostic about this at the moment. Thirdly, it's because I care about the Constitution and because I think it's necessary as far as possible to avoid risk. You have rightly quoted all the experts, but the experts, in saying that you constitutionalise the representations to executive government, cannot agree on whether or not that includes the Reserve Bank, Centrelink, the Great Barrier Reef Marine Park Authority or the Ombudsman, to quote Professor Davis's list of matters. So all I'm saying is: to avoid those sorts of ambiguities I think we can get it right. But that's not my call.

Senator WHITE: No, it isn't your call. I get back to my position about this. We've got to weigh up what these experts have said, and you are in the minority. Former chief justice Robert French has said that he doesn't see this as a barrier. He definitely has said that, and while I respect Senator Bragg and the other members of parliament, they've all got only one vote, like we do, in the end, too.

Father Brennan: Sure.

Senator WHITE: Can I just talk to you briefly about your experience of consulting with ministers of the Crown and also the bureaucracy. You were chief executive, weren't you, of the Catholic Social Services Australia from 2017 to 2021?

Father Brennan: I think those were about the dates—.

Senator WHITE: Or was it earlier than that?

Father Brennan: I think it would be earlier than that because this is my fourth year as Rector of Newman College, and I did the job of Catholic Social Services for, I think, three years.

Senator WHITE: But you were chief executive of Catholic Social Services Australia.

Father Brennan: I was.

Senator WHITE: When you started that position, you said that:

I intend to use my expertise and the lived experience of the tens of thousands of people who rely on services provided by the national network of Catholic social services to help our Federal politicians and bureaucrats to devise policies that assist those most in need.

In fact, you called out, as I said, federal politicians and bureaucrats as the people you were going to lobby and talk to. Over that period of your employment as the CEO of Catholic Social Services, did you meet with senior officials from departments of human services and social services—not just ministers—to lobby on behalf of those people in need?

Father Brennan: I did from time to time, yes.

Senator WHITE: Did you make representations to them so that you could influence government policy and outcomes?

Father Brennan: Sure. In fact, I remember specifically one of the issues which was alive at the time was that the then government was attempting the cashless debit card at Ceduna. We at Catholic Social Services had a large team at Ceduna, so I went to Ceduna and I met with the team there. Most of the team were Indigenous. I have to confess I had a slightly leftie Canberra view about the cashless debit card before I went to Ceduna, and I was opposed to it. But I got there and I heard that the majority of staff and the majority of clients actually thought it was a good thing. So it was those sorts of discussions that I then held with the minister and with senior bureaucrats.

Senator WHITE: You also made, didn't you, representations on the National Redress Scheme for institutional child sexual abuse?

Father Brennan: No. Not as far as I know.

Senator WHITE: No, you didn't? It wasn't one of the things that you talked about?

Father Brennan: No.

Senator WHITE: Okay. But you made these representations to senior officials because you assessed this as being an effective way of advancing the interests of Catholic Social Services agencies and the people who relied on the services; isn't that it? That Ceduna example is an example where the people that you represent had a different view. But you made those representations to bureaucrats and officials, didn't you?

Father Brennan: Absolutely. But I think the relevant distinction, if I may say so, is that I didn't have a special constitutional entitlement to do that. The question here is: do we want to set up a special constitutional entitlement for a constitutional entity to make representations to public servants? We're completely ad idem, aren't we, in that we want to be able to make those representations; the only point is whether there is a risk, by constitutionalising that part of it in clause 2, that clause 3 will not be able to eat clause 2?

Senator WHITE: Sure. But what we've heard from previous ministers for Indigenous affairs, as recently as last Friday, is that Aboriginal and Torres Strait Islander communities rarely get that opportunity. They don't have the same open-door access as you might of have had at Catholic Social Services.

Father Brennan: That's why we need a voice.

Senator WHITE: Yes. That's why they need a voice, but don't they need a voice at all levels, not just at one higher level, because sometimes, when it gets to the minister, it's all over red rover. My point to you is: why should you at Catholic Social Services have that open opportunity? What you're saying is that we shouldn't put that opportunity in the Constitution for Aboriginal and Torres Strait Islanders. They should be less effective than you were at Catholic Social Services.

Father Brennan: No. With respect, I think you've misheard me. I would say that I think Aboriginal people should have every entitlement, and more than my capacity, to make representations to all sorts of people.

Senator WHITE: Exactly.

Father Brennan: I think this parliament should provide for that. The only point of disagreement, as far as I can see, with respect, is whether or not you constitutionalise that part. Then what you do is you create the prospect. I mean, you quoted quite rightly justices

Hayne and French, who say you would not draw an implication that the voice would have an entitlement to know what the public servants were doing. You wouldn't draw an implication that they were allowed to have information sufficient to make an informed representation because—to quote Hayne—'you do not make implications in the Constitution that will bring government to a halt.' Or to quote French, 'to imply a duty to consult across all of that range would really make government unworkable.' Let's avoid all of that judicial carry-on and ensure, as you say, that Aboriginal people through the voice can be meaningful agitators and can be heard at all levels of government and at the Commonwealth level.

Senator WHITE: I have one more question. We have heard evidence that suggested that it will not happen at all levels unless it is in the Constitution and that putting it in the way that it has been framed, that it has been considered by advisory committee, is the best way to ensure it, because otherwise it won't happen. Do you concede that that is a possibility?

Father Brennan: Look, I don't pretend to be an expert in public administration. If you have had coherent evidence of that from departments then I concede.

Senator WHITE: We have heard it from former ministers.

Senator COX: Thank you, Father Brennan, for your work and for appearing today before the committee. I have a couple of questions. Along the campaigning lines, back on 10 April the Q&A program talked about faith, politics and humanity, and covered the breadth of issues in relation to faith. I want to draw on your experience in this context.

Father Brennan: Sorry, was that the program with Geraldine

Dougue and Senator Dodson?

Senator COX: No, it wasn't. It was Senator Payman and others.

Father Brennan: No I don't think that was me.

Senator COX: You might have to watch that one back. There is obviously a huge amount of history that First Nations people in this country have that is connected particularly to the church. Bringing faith along the journey with us in relation to the voice to parliament, can you talk a little bit about what you see your role in that being.

Father Brennan: Sure, with pleasure. Thank you for the question. One of the delights for me in the role that I am performing at the moment on this is I am working quite closely with what is called NATSICC, which is the Aboriginal and Torres Strait Islander Catholic Council. It is, if you like, the Indigenous voice to the Catholic Church. So I sat down in Adelaide the other day for 2½ hours. We did a splendid video with John Lochowiak, who is the chief executive of NATSICC. We had Aboriginal people, Aboriginal Catholic community members from around Australia zooming in with their questions and we had a Q&A type session. John and I will on Friday together jointly address the Catholic Bishops Conference of Australia on this issue.

As a church, as a social institution, like government generally, we are all learning slowly but it is about being attentive to those Indigenous voices and giving them a guaranteed place at the table. I have been very privileged to be engaged in that work for a long time. I might say, later in the month of May it is the 50th anniversary of Australian diplomatic relations with the Holy See. We have a very dynamic ambassador over there, Chiara Porro, and she is putting on a series of events in Reconciliation Week, where I will accompany Miriam-

Rose Ungunmerr-Baumann, a very splendid Aboriginal educator and artist from Nauiyu Nambiyu at Daly River. We will be there in Rome. We will meet personally with the Pope. We will give a couple of lectures together. That sort of participatory activity is actually central for us as a church now, and I think it helps to inform the passion I have for something like an Indigenous voice being recognised in the Constitution.

Senator COX: Do you think in your opinion that our current Constitution is fit for purpose given that in this program they actually talked about the majority of Australians being of non-faith denomination? In fact, people overwhelmingly now don't have a faith that they associate with themselves in Australia, yet we as parliamentarians still stand every morning for the reciting of the Lord's prayer. Do you think that it is not past time for us to update the Constitution but also to recognise in that the disparity that this has caused for First Nations people in this country?

Father Brennan: I do. I know that we are considering just the specific wording of your proposal at this stage but I did point out that I am one of those Australians who is disappointed that, even if this referendum is an overwhelming success, we are still going to have to the blight of section 25 in our Constitution, an absolutely outdated 19th-century provision. We are still going to have the blight of section 51(xxvi), about making special laws with respect to the people of a particular race for whom it is deemed necessary to make special laws. We should be ashamed as a nation. If I might say, you should be ashamed as a parliament that in the 21st-century we are going to amend the Australian Constitution without attending to those matters. Also, as I pointed out, as I move around the country, there is a great passion by a lot of Australians to see replicated something like that very good Aboriginal and Torres Strait Islander Recognition Act of 2013, which was passed by your parliament unanimously, acknowledging the fullness of Aboriginal history, Aboriginal present reality, Aboriginal future aspirations. I note he is giving evidence later today—Tony Abbott. All power to both Julia Gillard and Tony Abbott, who worked in a bipartisan fashion to have this parliament unanimously pass that. Why can't something like that be put an acknowledgement at the very beginning of our Constitution, not as a preamble, which will have Professor Craven and everyone upset about the effects, but just as a full fronted acknowledgement? So there are a lot of things in our Constitution which I think need to be improved and it is one of my regrets that simply by adding this chapter 9 and leaving unattended section 25, leaving unattended 51(xxvi) and leaving unattended a full acknowledgement of Indigenous history, I think, makes our Constitution, if I may say so, with respect, a bit of a dog's breakfast.

CHAIR: Thank you very much for appearing. Thank you for your detailed submission. We appreciate that.

3

Some of the proposed wording for the amendment to the Constitution

In May 2015, many of us turned our minds to what a constitutional provision for a Voice to Parliament might look like. I had written: 'At least in the first instance it would be impossible to design a constitutional provision for a council that was technically and legally sound, ensuring the untrammelled sovereignty of parliament'.[68] Professor Anne Twomey made a submission to the Joint Select Committee on Constitutional Recognition of Aboriginal and Torres Strait Islander Peoples. Taking up my challenge she put forward her first proposal for a constitutional provision. She foresaw the Voice having a fairly limited role with each piece of advice being tabled in Parliament and then considered by the Parliament when 'debating proposed laws with respect to Aboriginal and Torres Strait Islander peoples'.

The Referendum Council then got to work and the Uluru Dialogues occurred. After the publication of the Uluru Statement from the Heart, the three key convenors of the Dialogues put their suggested proposal to a new parliamentary committee co-chaired by Senator Patrick Dodson and Julian Leeser. Their proposal was much more broad ranging than Twomey's. They envisaged a Voice being able to make their views known to Parliament and to the government on any 'matters relating to Aboriginal and Torres Strait Islander peoples'. Anne Twomey then published her second proposal which was a truncated version of her first.

On election as prime minister, Anthony Albanese went to the Garma Festival and announced a slight variation of the proposal by the Uluru convenors as a conversation starter. I thought this proposal was overbroad, having no chance of acceptance by the Liberal Party and little prospect of success at a referendum.

Publishing the first edition of my book *An Indigenous Voice to Parliament: Building a Constitutional Bridge,* I suggested a formula which might have some prospect of acceptance by the Liberal Party (despite the National Party's antipathy) and which might appeal to voters concerned that the Constitution be colourblind, treating people of all races equally. My starting point was the constitutional fact that in the twenty first century, Aboriginal and Torres Strait Islander citizens were the only ones who would be subject to laws made under s.51(26) – laws with respect to the people of any race for whom it was deemed necessary to make special laws. Usually those laws would be made for the benefit of First Australians, but not necessarily. Sometimes those special laws would be measures judged by affected First Australians to be unacceptable and even detrimental. I thought the time had come when most Australians would agree that you should make special laws for a group on the basis of their race only if that group were first consulted and given the opportunity to provide advice. Such an approach should be especially commendable to the Liberal Party. If such an approach were adopted, there would be an increased chance of countering the simplistic argument that equality under the Constitution meant treating everyone the same. Given that First Australians were not treated the same, and ought not be treated the same when it came to laws such as land rights, native title and cultural heritage, there would continue to be a need for a constitutional provision empowering the Parliament to make special laws. The challenge was to design an appropriate consultative procedure for the making of such laws.

Noel Pearson had spoken of the Voice provision as a constitutional hook on which might hang other functions for the Voice. It seemed to me appropriate that the Voice have the constitutional function of being consulted and providing advice on proposed special laws and that the Voice be given additional functions defined in legislation, including the provision of advice and the making or representations to government, including public servants.

On 23 March 2023, before the establishment of any parliamentary committee to consider the proposed wording, Prime Minister Albanese held a press conference with key members of the Referendum Working Group announcing the proposed wording for the referendum. The government and the Referendum Working Group had no interest in considering any amendments on their merits. With no substantive change, these were the words that were then put to the Australian people on 14 October 2023.

Back on 31 May 2023, Julian Leeser, having resigned from the Opposition front bench and having committed himself to campaigning for a successful 'Yes' vote, unsuccessfully proposed amendments in the House of Representatives. He told the Parliament: '[M]y goal has been and is to put the constitutional alteration on a stronger electoral footing. I want to see the "yes" case win and win handsomely. Unfortunately, the polls indicate a downward trend, with support for the "yes" vote in the high 40s or low 50s. As I have been talking to people in my electorate and around Australia, I know there are Australians who are keen to vote "yes" but who are concerned about the wording of the alteration. These amendments are not about parliamentary colleagues; they're about securing the support of the Australian people—a majority of Australians and a majority of Australians in a majority of states. A successful referendum requires getting as many Australians as possible to vote "yes".'[69] But the government was not for turning, and the Opposition parties had no interest in amendments which might render the proposal more acceptable to voters on the more conservative side of politics.

Here is the wording of each of the proposals mentioned.

Anne Twomey, First Proposal, 20 May 2015[70]

Chapter 1A

60A(1) There shall be an Aboriginal and Torres Strait Islander body, to be called the [insert appropriate name, perhaps drawn from an Aboriginal or Torres Strait Islander language], which shall have the function of providing advice to the Parliament and the Executive Government on matters relating to Aboriginal and Torres Strait Islander peoples.

(2) The Parliament shall, subject to this Constitution, have power to make laws with respect to the composition, roles, powers and procedures of the [body].

(3) The Prime Minister [or the Speaker/President of the Senate] shall cause a copy of the [body's] advice to be tabled in each House of Parliament as soon as practicable after receiving it.

(4) The House of Representatives and the Senate shall give consideration to the tabled advice of the [body] in debating proposed laws with respect to Aboriginal and Torres Strait Islander peoples.

Megan Davis, Pat Anderson and Noel Pearson, 3 November 2018[71]

Chapter 9 First Nations

Section 129 The First Nations Voice

There shall be a First Nations Voice.

The First Nations Voice shall present its views to Parliament and the Executive on matters relating to Aboriginal and Torres Strait Islander peoples.

The Parliament shall, subject to this Constitution, have power to make laws with respect to the composition, functions, powers and procedures of the First Nations Voice.

Anne Twomey, 2nd Proposal, 8 July 2020[72]

The Commonwealth shall make provision for Aboriginal and Torres Strait Islander peoples to be heard by the Commonwealth regarding proposed laws and other matters with respect to Aboriginal and Torres Strait Islander affairs, and the Parliament may make laws to give effect to this provision.

Anthony Albanese, Garma Festival, 30 July 2022

There shall be a body, to be called the Aboriginal and Torres Strait Islander Voice.

The Aboriginal and Torres Strait Islander Voice may make representations to Parliament and the Executive Government on matters relating to Aboriginal and Torres Strait Islander Peoples.

The Parliament shall, subject to this Constitution, have power to make laws with respect to the composition, functions, powers and procedures of the Aboriginal and Torres Strait Islander Voice.

Frank Brennan, 22 February 2023[73]

Section 127

There shall be an Aboriginal and Torres Strait Islander Voice with such structure and functions as the Parliament deems necessary to facilitate consultation prior to the making of special laws with respect to Aboriginal and Torres Strait Islander peoples, and with such other functions as the Parliament determines.

Anthony Albanese, 23 March 2023[74]

Chapter IX Recognition of Aboriginal and Torres Strait Islander Peoples

129 Aboriginal and Torres Strait Islander Voice

In recognition of Aboriginal and Torres Strait Islander peoples as the First Peoples of Australia:

1. There shall be a body, to be called the Aboriginal and Torres Strait Islander Voice;

2. The Aboriginal and Torres Strait Islander Voice may make representations to the Parliament and the Executive Government of the Commonwealth on matters relating to Aboriginal and Torres Strait Islander peoples;

3. The Parliament shall, subject to this Constitution, have

power to make laws with respect to matters relating to the Aboriginal and Torres Strait Islander Voice, including its composition, functions, powers and procedures.

Julian Leeser, 31 May 2023[75]

Chapter IX - Recognition of Aboriginal and Torres Strait Islander Peoples

129 Aboriginal and Torres Strait Islander Voice

(i) There shall be a body, to be called the Aboriginal and Torres Strait Islander Voice;

(ii) The Parliament shall, subject to this Constitution, have power to make laws with respect to matters relating to the Aboriginal and Torres Strait Islander Voice, including its composition, functions, powers and procedures.

Provision put to the vote, 14 October 2023[76]

Chapter IX - Recognition of Aboriginal and Torres Strait Islander Peoples

129 Aboriginal and Torres Strait Islander Voice

In recognition of Aboriginal and Torres Strait Islander peoples as the First Peoples of Australia:

(i) there shall be a body, to be called the Aboriginal and Torres Strait Islander Voice;

(ii) the Aboriginal and Torres Strait Islander Voice may make representations to the Parliament and the Executive Government of the Commonwealth on matters relating to Aboriginal and Torres Strait Islander peoples;

(iii) the Parliament shall, subject to this Constitution, have power to make laws with respect to matters relating to the Aboriginal and Torres Strait Islander Voice, including its composition, functions, powers and procedures.

4

Notes on Justiciability

Clause 2 of the proposed amendment provided that the 'Voice may make representations to the Parliament and the Executive Government of the Commonwealth on matters relating to Aboriginal and Torres Strait Islander peoples'. So this would include not only representations to Parliament on proposed laws and to ministers on policies and practices, but also representations to public servants whenever they were making decisions which could impact Aboriginal or Torres Strait Islander persons. This would include much more than those decisions impacting exclusively or especially on First Australians. Any public servant making a decision having an impact on an Aboriginal person could be required to receive representations from the Voice. Advocates for the amendment said there was nothing to fear as clause 3 provided that the Parliament had the 'power to make laws with respect to matters relating to the Aboriginal and Torres Strait Islander Voice, including its composition, functions, powers and procedures'. These advocates were not troubled that clause 3 was specified to be 'subject to this Constitution', and therefore unable to limit the scope of clause 2. So there was a lot of background discussion going on about the 'justiciability' of these representations and decisions. I circulated five notes on justiciability.

The first note drew extensively on Robert French's comprehensive paper 'Constitutional Review of Executive Decisions – Australia's US Legacy', delivered at the John Marshall Law School under the auspices of the Chicago Bar Association.[77] The second note was a response to French's article with Geoffrey Lindell published in the *Australian Financial Review* the previous day.[78] The third note was a response to French's observations to me. The fourth note was circulated to key individuals in the week of the launch of the first edition of my book *An Indigenous Voice to Parliament: Seeking a Constitutional Bridge*. It followed upon the very detailed interview I did with Michelle Grattan highlighting the problem with the wording.[79] The fifth note was a response to Robert French's article in *The Australian* on 13 July 2023.[80] It is appropriate in the interests of transparency that these notes now be published unamended.

1ˢᵗ Note on Justiciability

1 February 2023

In this note, I will refer only to the utterances of past and present High Court judges.

On 30 July 2023, Prime Minister Albanese proposed these words for insertion in the Constitution:

1. There shall be a body, to be called the Aboriginal and Torres Strait Islander Voice.

2. The Aboriginal and Torres Strait Islander Voice may make representations to Parliament and the Executive Government on matters relating to Aboriginal and Torres Strait Islander Peoples.

3. The Parliament shall, subject to this Constitution, have power to make laws with respect to the composition, functions, powers and procedures of the Aboriginal and Torres Strait Islander Voice.

In 2019, ex Chief Justice Murray Gleeson who had been a member of the Referendum Council delivered an address which was posited on the Voice being only a Voice to Parliament, and chiefly on proposed laws made under s.51(26).[81] That had always been my understanding of the import of Recommendation 1 of the Referendum Council's Final Report.

The High Court would be very wary about interfering with parliamentary processes. There would be little likelihood of the High Court judicially reviewing the processes of parliament or the content of a proposed Bill on the grounds that the Parliament had failed to give due regard to a representation received from the Voice. Or to put it another way, there would be little prospect of the High Court stipulating the requirements for a communication from the Voice to the parliament to be classified as a representation.

Representations to the Executive government are an altogether different matter.

Executive government includes ministers and public servants. Representations could relate to policy questions or to administrative decisions.

Especially in migration cases, the High Court has developed an elaborate jurisprudence ensuring that decisions by Executive government can be reviewed by the courts even when parliament has legislated a privative clause purporting to exclude all judicial review. Even with the application of a privative clause, the courts remain free to interfere with a purported executive decision affected by jurisdictional error. Justice Gageler when Solicitor General put it well when he said, invoking Chief Justice Murray Gleeson, that 'an entitlement at least to the observance of fair procedures in administrative decision-making should now be treated as one of the "basic rights of the individual" which is not to be taken away by statute in the absence of express language or necessary implication'[82]. Gageler said, 'Keeping administrative decision-makers within the express limits of the lawful authority given to them by statute is as uncontroversial as it is mechanical. Keeping administrative decision-makers within the limits that are implied into the terms by which lawful authority is given to them by statute is more problematic.'[83]

Chief Justice French pithily described to a Chicago audience the effect of the S157 v The Commonwealth decision on which the full bench including Justice Hayne sat: In '*Plaintiff S157 v The Commonwealth*[84] the Court held that the privative clause did not oust the jurisdiction because it did not extend to decisions affected by jurisdictional error. Such decisions were only purported decisions. They were not decisions made under the Act.'

French CJ said: 'A failure to comply with conditions or restraints upon the exercise of statutory powers which vitiates the purported exercise of such powers, would amount to jurisdictional error. ... It might also be failure to comply with the requirements of procedural fairness.'[85]

French told his American audience, 'Examples of jurisdictional error which illustrate that point include error of law which causes the decision-maker to identify a wrong issue, ask itself a wrong question, ignore relevant material or rely upon irrelevant material and, in some circumstances, to make an erroneous finding or reach a mistaken conclusion which causes it to exceed its authority or powers.'

French went on to say:

> 'Other matters constituting jurisdictional error may include bad faith or a breach of the rules of procedural fairness on the part of the decision-maker. The rules of procedural fairness broadly require that unless excluded by the relevant statute a person to be affected adversely by a decision has an opportunity to be heard before the decision is made and to comment on or respond to material before the decision-maker which may lead to an adverse outcome. They also involve a requirement that the decision-maker be impartial in the sense that there is no actual or ostensible bias against the person affected. The

rules are seen as an implied limitation of the grant of power to the decision-maker. That is unless the implication is excluded by express words or perhaps a necessary contrary implication.'

But of course, there could be no prospect of a statute working implied or express exclusion of the requirement of 'procedural fairness' whatever that might be in the case of a decision maker's consideration of a representation from the Voice. No statute could pare back the constitutional requirements (whatever they may be) for appropriate reception of a representation received from the Voice.

What then would be the High Court's approach not to a statute setting limits on a public servant's requirement to observe fair procedures when making a decision relating to an individual (even a non-citizen), but to a constitutional provision requiring a public servant to receive representations from a constitutional entity (the Voice) having the constitutional entitlement to make representations about any matter relating to Aboriginal and Torres Strait Islander Peoples?

Even before getting to the High Court's capacity to imply requirements (a la *Love* and *Thoms*, where the court implied words of limitation on the 'aliens' head of power), we need to consider that a constitutional entitlement of the Voice to make representations entails a constitutional requirement for public servants or ministers to receive and consider representations. The constitutional requirement (the incidents of which could be determined only by the High Court) could not be excluded, limited or abridged by statute, implicitly or even explicitly.

In one migration case last year, the High Court had cause to consider the decision maker's approach to representations. In *Plaintiff M1-2021 v Minister for Home Affairs*, Kiefel CJ, Keane, Gordon and

Steward JJ. said:[86]

'23 [T]he decision-maker cannot ignore the representations. The question remains how the representations are to be considered.

'24 Consistently with well-established authority in different statutory contexts, there can be no doubt that a decision-maker must read, identify, understand and evaluate the representations. Adopting and adapting what Kiefel J (as her Honour then was) said in Tickner v Chapman, the decision-maker must have regard to what is said in the representations, bring their mind to bear upon the facts stated in them and the arguments or opinions put forward, and appreciate who is making them. From that point, the decisionmaker might sift them, attributing whatever weight or persuasive quality is thought appropriate. The weight to be afforded to the representations is a matter for the decision-maker. And the decision-maker is not obliged "to make actual findings of fact as an adjudication of all material claims" made by a former visa holder.

'25 It is also well-established that the requisite level of engagement by the decision-maker with the representations must occur within the bounds of rationality and reasonableness. What is necessary to comply with the statutory requirement for a valid exercise of power will necessarily depend on the nature, form and content of the representations. The requisite level of engagement – the degree of effort needed by the decision-maker – will vary, among other things, according to the length, clarity and degree of relevance of the representations. The decision-maker is not required to consider claims that are not clearly articulated or which do not clearly arise on the materials before them.

'26 Labels like "active intellectual process" and "proper, genuine and realistic consideration" must be understood in their proper context. These formulas have the danger of creating "a kind of general warrant, invoking language of indefinite and subjective application, in which the procedural and substantive merits of any [decisionmaker's] decision can be scrutinised". That is not the correct approach. As Mason J stated in *Minister for Aboriginal Affairs v Peko-Wallsend Ltd*, "[t]he limited role of a court reviewing the exercise of an administrative discretion must constantly be borne in mind". The court does not substitute its decision for that of an administrative decision-maker.

'27 None of the preceding analysis detracts from, or is inconsistent with, established principle that, for example, if review of a decisionmaker's reasons discloses that the decisionmaker ignored, overlooked or misunderstood relevant facts or materials or a substantial and clearly articulated argument; misunderstood the applicable law; or misunderstood the case being made by the former visa holder, that may give rise to jurisdictional error.'

This case like most migration cases related to a non-citizen, not to a citizen, and definitely not to a constitutional entity. This case related to a reasonable expectation of having a representation considered by the decision maker when that reasonable expectation has not been displaced by statute (express or implied). How would the High Court adapt its reasoning for a constitutional entity having a constitutional entitlement to make representations? Undoubtedly the court would be more, rather than less, demanding of decision makers.

A constitutional entity with a constitutional entitlement to make representations on any matter relating to Aboriginal and Torres Strait Islander Peoples would have standing in the High Court to seek relief under s.75(v) against any minister or public servant who failed to accord the appropriate level of constitutional consideration of those representations.

Callinan must surely be right when he says, 'Stretching my imagination only a little, I would foresee a decade or more of constitutional and administrative law litigation arising out of a voice whether constitutionally entrenched or not. Every state and territory is likely to have an interest in any representations and in the interactions between the voice and the constitutionally entrenched houses of parliament and executive government.'[87] I do not share Hayne's nonchalance about the prospects of future litigation.[88] I do think Callinan's concerns would be manageable if the Voice's representations to Executive Government were the subject of parliamentary enactment rather than of constitutional entitlement.

I am a strong advocate for the Voice, and I think it needs to be able to deal with government as well as parliament. But we need a constitutional provision which retains the parliament's capacity to limit the consideration due from ministers and public servants to any representation received from the Voice, or any (dissenting) member of the Voice.

I remain hopeful that the parliament will set up a committee for the receipt of suggestions, the recommendation of options, and the publication of detailed advice on justiciability from the Solicitor General.

2nd Note on Justiciability

A comment on French and Lindell, 'Voice is low risk but high return'

Australian Financial Review

5 February 2023[89]

A good piece overall, but in my opinion, one key error, with all respect to the very learned authors. They state:

> 'The function of the Voice is set out in the second part of the amendment. To "make representations" is to make official statements to the parliament and the executive. Those words cover submissions or advice about existing or proposed laws and administrative policies and practices. There is no constitutional legal obligation to accept or be bound by such submissions or advice. There would, however, be a high democratic obligation to respect them and take them into account.'

For completeness, they should state: 'Those words cover submissions or advice about existing or proposed laws and administrative policies and practices – with which there may be little prospect of litigation.

'But those words also cover submissions or advice about administrative decisions made by public servants which impact on the claimed entitlement of Aboriginal and Torres Strait Islander citizens – and there is every prospect of their litigating their claims under s.75(v).'

The problem with clause 2 of the Garma formula is that it not only provides a constitutional entity (the Voice) with a constitutional entitlement to make representations to ministers on matters of policy, it also provides that constitutional entity with the constitutional entitlement to make representations to public servants on matters relating to ATSI when those public servants will be making a final administrative decision impacting the right or interests of ATSI under the law.

Consider just a couple of examples.

A public servant is to make a final administrative decision under the *Environment Protection and Biodiversity Conservation Act* relating to ATSI interests. The Voice makes a representation about the proposed approval for mining (say). The Voice is dissatisfied with the manner in which the public servant has considered the Voice's representation.

One other example. *The Australian Education Act 2013* is the main legislation for Commonwealth funding to government and non-government schools.

The Act sets out:

- The rights and responsibilities of organisations in order for them to receive Australian Government funding for school education

- Broad expectations for compliance, to ensure funding accountability to the Commonwealth and school communities.

The Voice makes a representation to the relevant public servant about the funding of Aboriginal schools in remote communities, or about the preconditions for approval to conduct such schools. The Voice, or perhaps only a dissenting member of the Voice, or perhaps a regional Voice which plugs into the national Voice is dissatisfied with the final decision which has been made impacting a citizen's right or interests under the law, just this time 'the citizen' is a group of citizens who are a constitutional entity with a constitutional entitlement to make representations. Thus s.75(v) litigation is a real prospect.

To put it another way, French and Lindell assume (and presumably would insist) that the Voice never make representations to a public servant about a pending administrative decision which would determine some Indigenous entitlement. Otherwise there'd be review under s.75(v).

The Voice will have to be confined to representations on policies and practices, excluding administrative decisions.

You will note that the authors state:

> '[T]here is little or no scope for any court to find constitutional legal obligations in the amendment. And if parliament made a law which created unintended opportunities for challenges to executive action, the law could be adjusted.'

But parliament will not be able to make a law excluding already existing constitutional entitlement to challenge executive action.

The authors throughout the article presume that representations to Executive governments are restricted to matters of policy and practice, rather than actual executive decisions for the benefit or detriment of ATSI.

French and Lindell go on to say:

> 'That said, there is little or no scope for any court to find constitutional legal obligations in the amendment. And if parliament made a law which created unintended opportunities for challenges to executive action, the law could be adjusted. There are many examples of that.'

> 'A law providing that the executive was required to take into

account representations from the Voice as a condition of the exercise of executive power would, in all probability, be justiciable. If parliament imposed such a requirement, the executive must be held to account if it does not comply with it. But in providing for representations to be made to the executive, the law does not have to impose such a requirement. That is a matter for the parliament.'

They overlook that the Garma formula would already provide a constitutional requirement that the executive be required to take into account representations from the Voice as a condition of the exercise of executive power, and that this would be justiciable. And it would not be possible for Parliament to withdraw that requirement.

Thus the need for a constitutional amendment that does not include the constitutional entitlement to make representations on 'the exercise of executive power', but which allows the parliament, should it wish, to allow some power for the Voice to make representations on 'the exercise of executive power' and not just on general matters of policy and practice. See endnote for Callinan's article 'Examining the case for the voice – an argument against.'[90]

3rd Note on Justiciability[91]

8 February 2023

What say you enacted a provision:

> 1. The Aboriginal and Torres Strait Islander Voice may make representations to Executive Government on administrative decisions relating to Aboriginal and Torres Strait Islander Peoples.

Would not the Voice be able to seek prerogative relief under s.75(v) on all the usual grounds of jurisdictional error etc?

So what is the case when you enact a provision:

> The Aboriginal and Torres Strait Islander Voice may make representations to Parliament and the Executive Government on matters relating to Aboriginal and Torres Strait Islander Peoples.

Would not the Voice still be able to seek prerogative relief under s.75(v) in relation to administrative decisions by public servants on all the usual grounds of jurisdictional error etc, regardless of the fact that prerogative relief would not be available in relation to representations to Parliament or representations to Executive government on policy matters?

Is it not a case of: If prerogative relief is available in relation to 'A', then it remains available even if the body is entitled to make representations not just in relation to 'A' but also in relation to 'B' and

'C' which do not attract prerogative relief, and in the same way as if the body was entitled to make representations only in relation to 'A'?

If a constitutional entitlement to make representations to the executive decision maker is conferred is that not an opportunity for the Voice to be heard by that decision maker on the making of that representation? And if so, why wouldn't the content of the requirements of natural justice in the decision making process be justiciable?

Furthermore, if you enacted a constitutional provision: 'The Aboriginal and Torres Strait Islander Voice may make representations to Executive Government on administrative decisions relating to Aboriginal and Torres Strait Islander Peoples', the parliament could not legislate to limit access to prerogative relief to review whether there was jurisdictional error etc in the receipt of the representations by public servants.

4th Note on Justiciability

24 February 2023

This is the fourth in a series of notes on justiciability not intended for publication but circulated to those inquiring about my view on the contested issue of justiciability in the Garma formula.

The first note (1/2) drew extensively on Robert French's comprehensive paper 'Constitutional Review of Executive Decisions –Australia's US Legacy', John Marshall Law School – Chicago Bar Association. The second note (5/2) was a response to French's article with Lindell published in the *AFR* the previous day.[92] The third note (8/2) was a response to French's observations to me.

I started writing these notes because the advice from the Constitutional Expert Group published by Minister Burney on 22 December 2022 failed to address the question of justiciability.[93] However next day, Professor George Williams a member of the Constitutional Expert Group had published an op ed in *The Australian* stating:

'There is no requirement that the voice be listened to before a decision being made. Decisions can be made without the voice having its say, and indeed the voice could be ignored if parliament and the executive decide to do so.

'The answer would be different if the wording said the voice must be consulted, but it does not do so. To suggest otherwise is to read words into the amendment that are not there.'

See article in *The Australian*: 'Expert stress tests show the voice is not a threat'.[94]

One was left with the impression that this was the unanimous view of the Constitutional Expert Group. But was this correct? And just as importantly for any referendum campaign, was this view adequately certain and beyond reasonable contestation?

One can see how far the ground has moved on these two questions simply by considering George Williams' latest op ed on the matter published on 21/2:

> 'We expect that people who exercise public power on behalf of the community will make fair decisions following a sound process.

> 'This includes taking into account information relevant to making the decision. If a public official fails to consider important information of this kind, courts routinely direct that person to go back and make the decision again, taking into account the information that was missed. The court does not direct what the decision should be, only that it is properly made.

> 'The upshot is that ministers who receive a representation from the voice may need to read and consider that representation when they make a decision. For example, if a minister is considering whether to impose an alcohol ban on an Indigenous community, and the voice had made representations about whether this was a sound idea and what the impact on the community would be, the minister should take this into account. If the minister refused to read advice from the voice, someone might go to court to ask the minister to remake the decision with the benefit of all the relevant information.

> 'This is the system working as it should. The rule of law and independent oversight by judges should apply to the voice as they do to every other government body. The voice must operate within its limits, and representations by the voice should be taken into account when making decisions that

affect Indigenous people.'

See article in *The Australian*: 'Expect the courts to play a role in operation of voice'.[95]

What then is the view of the Constitutional Expert Group? Other press reports seem to indicate they are not unanimous.

At the National Press Club, the day after the publication of the latest Williams piece, this exchange took place:

'JOURNALIST: Prime Minister, you said you want to reach across the aisle over the Voice. I might have something that might help you with it. Father Frank Brennan, respected Jesuit priest, Professor in law, a huge advocate for Indigenous Australians, a very strong supporter of the Voice, but he does not believe that the draft amendment — and you said it was a draft, is water tight, legally. He's put forward in this book he's released this week, 'An Indigenous Voice to Parliament: Considering a Constitutional Bridge', he believes a tighter and a clearer amendment that he thinks is water tight. You've got this Senate committee kicking off next month, it's going to receive public submissions like Father Frank's. You said that it is a draft. Are you open to change?

'PRIME MINISTER: We've actually got a constitutional working group that is working through these issues, including former High Court Judge Justice Hayne, Including Professor Twomey, a range of constitutional experts all working through these issues. Father Frank Brennan, he is a friend of mine, he has my utmost respect and he is someone who is a very good person and actually sat on, the thing about this process is on the Calma-Langton review wasn't just Calma-Langton. Professor Brennan was a part of it, Chris Kenny, a whole range of people were a part of that process as well that came and fed into the Calma-Langton review. I think that the advice, and with due respect to Frank who does have my respect on legal matters, I look at article in the *Australian Financial Review* by the former Chief Justice French was, in my view, a really clear outline of why these issues are very, very tight in the draft wording which is there. But I'm open to, I don't have a closed mind on these things but I think that the constitutional working group that's been established is working through these issues as well.' See press club speech.[96]

Bob French had further expanded his public explanation of justiciability in his address to the Gilbert and Tobin Constitutional Conference on 10/2 entitled 'Commentary on Climate Change Litigation and Voice Presentations'. These are the key paragraphs:

'11. There has been an argument floated that the proposed amendment might give rise to a constitutional implication that representations made by The Voice to the Executive Government could be mandatory, relevant considerations in executive decision-making which could be challenged in the courts if consideration had not been given to an applicable representation.

'12. This would appear to be a highly improbable scenario for the following reasons:

'(1) The wording of paragraph 2 of the amendment encompasses representations to the Parliament. They cannot bear an implication that the Parliament is bound to have regard to them as a legal condition of its law-making powers.

'(2) The range of matters in which representations could be made to the Executive would include many matters of policy of the kind that Allsop CJ in *Sharma* described as 'core policy' and on any view outside the purview of the judiciary.

'(3) An implication of the kind floated would have to carve out of the enormous range of matters upon which representations could be made to the Executive, matters in which an executive officer or body is exercising a statutory or non-statutory power. It would have to attach to those matters consideration of the representation as a condition of the valid exercise of the power. Paragraph 2 simply states what The Voice may do and does so at the highest level of generality. The spectre of litigation based on a significant but narrow cast constitutional implication unstated but lurking within those words, is a shadow which distracts from the substantive debate.

'13. There is always the possibility that someone, someday would want to litigate matters relating to The Voice as can anybody who seeks recourse to the courts. That flows from the fact that we are a country governed by the rule of law which provides access to the courts where it is said that public officials have exceeded their power. That said there is little or no scope to find constitutional, legal obligations in the facilitative and empowering provisions of the amendment.

'14. If the Parliament wanted to it could make a law providing that the exercise of defined statutory or non-statutory executive power would be conditioned upon consideration of relevant representations from The Voice. And if Parliament imposed such a requirement, the exercise of the power would be judicially reviewable if it were not complied with. There is, however, no obligation to impose such a condition. That would be a matter for the Parliament.'

My problem is with paragraph 14.

Tracing through French's logic and applying it to the Garma formula:

What happens if the Constitution as interpreted by the High Court 'creates unintended opportunities for challenges to executive action'? You can't go and 'adjust' the Constitution.

French readily concedes (as the Constitutional Expert Group did not, before Christmas): 'A law providing that the Executive was required to take into account representations from The Voice as a condition of the exercise of executive power would, in all probability, be justiciable.'

If the Constitution imposed such a requirement, the Executive must be held to account if it does not comply with it.

And with the Garma formula, the Constitution does impose such a requirement. It is no longer a matter for Parliament.

Thus the need to get back to basics with Recommendation 1 of the Referendum Council as faithfully enunciated by Murray Gleeson.

The Garma formula needs to be amended either by (a) omitting the constitutional entitlement of the Voice to make representations to ministers and public servants on policies, practices and administrative decisions in any way related to Aboriginal and Torres Strait Islander peoples; or (b) explicitly restricting that constitutional entitlement in a way which would satisfy both departmental heads that the workings of government would not be unduly clogged and the Solicitor-General (and AGD and AGS) that the decisions of public servants would not be unnecessarily subject to judicial review.

There would of course be no problem with parliament by statute deciding the extent to which Parliament wanted the Voice to be able to make representations to ministers and public servants on policies, practices and administrative decisions in any way related to Aboriginal and Torres Strait Islander peoples. Unintended problems which then arose with public administration or judicial review could be considered by Parliament.

My suggested amendment would, I am sure, be just one of many were there to be a parliamentary committee in existence to which we could make submissions.

5th Note on Justiciability

30 August 2023

On 13 July 2023, Robert French published an opinion piece 'Parliament will add flesh to voice skeleton' in which he said:[97]

> 'It has been suggested that the proposed amendment might give rise to a constitutional implication that representations made by the voice to the executive government could be mandatory considerations in executive decision-making, which could be challenged in the courts if consideration had not been given to an applicable representation. This is an improbable scenario. Subsection 129 (ii) cannot bear an implication that the parliament is bound to have regard to representations as a legal condition of its lawmaking powers.

> 'The great range of matters in which representations could be made to the executive government would include many matters of policy that are, on any view, outside the scope of judicial review. No such implication is likely to be applied to them. How then could it be applied to a small subset of executive decision-making that involves the judicially reviewable exercise of legal powers or discretions? The parliament can make laws under subsection 129 (iii) that provide for the legal effect of representations to the executive government. That is inconsistent with a constitutional implication determining the legal effect of voice representations.'

What say the parliament were to legislate for a Voice which could make representations to public servants making administrative decisions relating to Aboriginal and Torres Strait Islander peoples. Would not the High Court following the usual administrative law jurisprudence find an implication that public servants in such a situation would be required to give notice to the Voice when intending to make such a decision and to provide sufficient information so that the Voice might make an informed representation prior to the making of such a decision?

If so, why would the situation be any different in relation to the Voice with a constitutional entitlement to make such representations? It is nothing to the point that the same implications would not be drawn in relation to representations being made to parliament or to ministers in relation to policy questions. They are qualitatively quite different and readily distinguishable.

One need only consider *Minister for Immigration v SZSSJ*, in which seven judges, including French CJ, said:[98]

> 'Ordinarily, affording a reasonable opportunity to be heard in the exercise of a statutory power to conduct an inquiry requires that a person whose interest is apt to be affected be put on notice of: the nature and purpose of the inquiry; the issues to be considered in conducting the inquiry, and the nature and content of information that the repository of power undertaking the inquiry might take into account as a reason for coming to a conclusion adverse to the person.'

Despite French's assertion, the matter of the legal effect of representations made by the voice to the executive government would not be resolved simply by determining whether it is a case of mandatory considerations in executive decision-making. When considering a decision maker's approach to representations, Kiefel CJ, Keane, Gordon and Steward JJ provide some guidance about the broad scope of matters to be considered in *Plaintiff M1/2021 v Minister for Home Affairs* [2022] HCA 17; 96 ALJR 497 at [22]-[27]. The scope goes well beyond what might be classified as 'mandatory relevant considerations':

'22 Section 501CA(4) of the *Migration Act* confers a wide discretionary power on a decisionmaker to revoke a decision to cancel a visa held by a noncitizen if satisfied that there is "another reason" why that decision should be revoked. The statutory scheme for determining whether the decision-maker is satisfied that there is "another reason" for revoking a cancellation decision commences with a former visa holder making representations. In determining whether they are satisfied that there is "another reason" for revoking a cancellation decision, the decisionmaker undertakes the assessment by reference to the case made by the former visa holder by their representations.

'23 It is, however, improbable that Parliament intended for that broad discretionary power to be restricted or confined by requiring the decision-maker to treat every statement within representations made by a former visa holder as a mandatory relevant consideration. But the decision-maker cannot ignore the representations. The question remains how the representations are to be considered.

'24 Consistently with well-established authority in different statutory contexts, there can be no doubt that a decision-maker must read, identify, understand and evaluate the representations. Adopting and adapting what Kiefel J (as her Honour then was) said in *Tickner v Chapman*, the decision-maker must have regard to what is said in the representations, bring their mind to bear upon the facts stated in them and the arguments or opinions put forward, and appreciate who is making them. From that point, the decisionmaker might sift them, attributing whatever weight or persuasive quality is thought appropriate. The weight to be afforded to the representations is a matter for the decision-maker. And the decision-maker is not obliged "to make actual findings of fact as an adjudication of all material claims" made by a former visa holder.

'25 It is also well-established that the requisite level of engagement by the decision-maker with the representations must occur within the bounds of rationality and reasonableness. What is necessary to comply with the statutory requirement for a valid exercise of power will necessarily depend on the nature, form and content of the representations. The requisite level of engagement – the degree of effort needed by the decision-maker – will vary, among other things, according to the length, clarity and degree of relevance of the representations. The decision-maker is not required to consider claims that are not clearly articulated or which do not clearly arise on the materials before them.

'26 Labels like "active intellectual process" and "proper, genuine and realistic consideration" must be understood in their proper context. These formulas have the danger of creating "a kind of general warrant, invoking language of indefinite and subjective application, in which the procedural and substantive merits of any [decisionmaker's] decision can be scrutinised". That is not the correct approach. As Mason J stated in *Minister for Aboriginal Affairs v Peko-Wallsend Ltd*, "[t]he limited role of a court reviewing the exercise of an administrative discretion must constantly be borne in mind". The court does not substitute its decision for that of an administrative decision-maker.

'27 None of the preceding analysis detracts from, or is inconsistent with, established principle that, for example, if review of a decisionmaker's reasons discloses that the decisionmaker ignored, overlooked or misunderstood relevant facts or materials or a substantial and clearly articulated argument; misunderstood the applicable law; or misunderstood the case being made by the former visa holder, that may give rise to jurisdictional error.'

Even if the parliament, subject to the Constitution, has power to make laws under s.129(iii), that power could not extend to negating the Voice's legal entitlement to receive reasonable notice of an intention to make an administrative decision relating to Aboriginal and Torres Strait Islander peoples and to make informed representations to public servants in relation to same pursuant to s.129(ii). Contrary to the assertion of French, this is anything but an 'improbable scenario'. This can hardly be classified as a 'small subset of executive decision-making that involves the judicially reviewable exercise of legal powers or discretions'. It would be a substantial subset of executive decision making which, like all other executive decision making, would attract judicially reviewable exercise of legal powers or discretions.

French seems to be arguing that s.129(iii) is broad enough to permit complete negation of an entitlement to notice or information prior to the making of an administrative decision relating to Aboriginal and Torres Strait Islander peoples. Presumably he and Hayne would advocate such legislation to avoid the clogging of the workings of government. But, as ever, this brings us back to the problem highlighted by David Jackson KC in para 7 of his submission:

'Greater potential difficulty is provided by the phrase "subject to this Constitution" in proposed s 129(3). That usage would ordinarily cause no difficulty, but one provision which would be likely to fall within it would be the proposed s 129(2). If a law made pursuant to s 129(3) had the effect that the Voice (however constituted under s 129(3)) was not empowered to make a representation of the nature referred to in s 129(2), the relevant provisions enacted pursuant to s 129(2)[99] would be invalid.'

Conclusion

Since the disastrous referendum result, Labor stalwarts with a strong commitment to Indigenous rights like Paul Keating and Peter Garrett have publicly lamented the basic errors made during the 2023 campaign. Several Aboriginal leaders who were members of the government's handpicked Referendum Advisory Group have admitted that there was a need for a more inclusive process and for more precise wording of the proposed change to the Constitution.

Celebrating his 80th birthday, Paul Keating gave a broad ranging interview in the Financial Review published on 21 February 2024, declaring that the Voice referendum was 'a mistake from the start'. He disclosed that he had told Marcia Langton and Megan Davis back in 2016 that he opposed the constitutional route. He said, 'A lot of clever Aboriginal people have wasted a lot of years on this issue'.[100] Responding to the interview, Marcia Langton said: 'Paul Keating was right. We should have proceeded to legislate the Voice concept of regional Indigenous representation and joint decision-making before a referendum.'[101] Mick Gooda repeated his criticism of the 'crash or crash through' approach adopted by Mr Albanese and key Indigenous advisers like Noel Pearson who, during the campaign, had attacked Gooda as a 'bedwetter' for wanting to investigate alternative wording of the referendum proposal.

Shortly thereafter, Peter Garrett's observations were published in The Weekend Australian. He thought it was 'a very disappointing result, particularly for Aboriginal people who had championed the Voice – but not entirely unexpected, given the fact that it was opposed very early on by the alternative prime minister.' Garrett observed: 'Mr Dutton's act was highly regrettable. Mr Albanese probably in hindsight should have said, "If we don't have the support of the Opposition leader, it's pretty clear that it can't succeed." He didn't want to disappoint many people who felt that it should have been put anyway, including the indigenous leadership. That was probably a mistake in hindsight.'[102]

When putting my own suggested wording for the constitutional change back in February 2023, I was not claiming the legal acumen to decide singlehandedly the ideal wording of the Constitution. I was putting forward a suggestion which I thought was consistent with the architecture of the Constitution, consistent with what had been proposed by the Referendum Council in 2017, and consistent with the limits on the Voice which its proponents were claiming could be imposed by the Parliament.

My suggestion was a new section 127 of the Constitution:

> 'There shall be an Aboriginal and Torres Strait Islander Voice with such structure and functions as the Parliament deems necessary to facilitate consultation prior to the making of special laws with respect to Aboriginal and Torres Strait Islander peoples, and with such other functions as the Parliament determines.'

By putting this suggestion, I was hoping to pressure the Albanese government to widen its circle of consultation, providing at the very least a transparent parliamentary committee process open to recommending changes to the wording. I was also hoping to pressure members of the Liberal Party to come on board with a tighter provision which would be seen to be more consistent with the Liberal Party's philosophical approach and objections, insofar as such objections were philosophical and not simply the result of a deliberately negative spoiling strategic approach to being in Opposition.

In February and March 2023, I was at pains to make clear to government that my legal concern with the wording was not so much the legal effect of government decisions made without appropriate consultation with the Voice, but with the legal effect of claims made by the Voice prior to the making of any government decisions relating to Aboriginal and Torres Strait Islander persons. Could the Voice glue up the system of government by asking the courts to direct public servants to give notice to the Voice prior to the making of any relevant decisions? And could the Voice further glue up the system of government by asking for those public servants to provide sufficient information prior to the making of any decision so as to allow the Voice to make a reasoned representation? And could this glueing up occur even if Parliament were able to legislate that public servants give minimal, if any, consideration to Voice representations once made? I thought it essential that the Solicitor General be asked to advise on these questions and that his advice be tabled in the Parliament. The government declined to do so, assuring us that there was no problem despite the advice of lawyers (far more experienced than me) that the problems were real and insurmountable.

Instead of asking the Solicitor General to advise on the legal requirements for public servants to provide notice and relevant information to the Voice prior to the making of relevant decisions, the government simply asked him to advise on the fairly uncontested question:

> 'Would the power to legislate "with respect to matters relating to the Aboriginal and Torres Strait Islander Voice" in proposed s 129(iii) of the Constitution empower the Parliament to specify whether, and if so, how, Executive Government decision-makers are legally required to consider relevant representations of the Voice?'[103]

In effect, the Solicitor General rightly advised that the Parliament had the power under proposed s.129(iii) to order public servants to disregard or give only the most perfunctory consideration to any representations received from the Voice. But because he was not asked, he gave no advice on whether Parliament had the power to overrule the constitutional entitlement of the Voice to make the representations in the first place. Absent a valid legislative provision, the Voice would always be entitled to receive notice of a pending decision and sufficient information to make a reasoned representation prior to the making of the decision. That's just basic administrative law. This would be the case even if Parliament enacted a valid provision permitting public servants to disregard or give the most fleeting consideration to Voice representations once received. While the Solicitor General was focused on the legal effect of public service decisions after any representations had been made by the Voice, I was focused on the legal effect of public service neglect or non-transparency prior to the making of representations by the Voice. They were completely different questions. The first was agreed and non-controversial; the second was contested and very controversial.

I thought it worthwhile to agitate for my amendment when 2GB talk back radio host Ben Fordham gave it his backing.[104] But once the government indicated its intransigence with the announcement of its proposed wording on 23 March 2023 (prior to the setting up of the parliamentary committee), I abandoned my proposed amendment and suggested that the government's proposal be tweaked to provide that the Voice's constitutional entitlement to make representations be confined to Parliament and ministers rather than to Parliament, ministers and public servants. By then, the Liberal Party had joined its junior coalition partner, the National Party, in opposing the referendum. Very few sitting Liberals were lured across into the Yes camp. All was lost.

Back in August 2022, Malcolm Turnbull had changed his position and committed himself to a 'Yes' vote. But privately, he maintained his political analysis that there was never any prospect of the referendum getting up. Five months after the referendum, Lech Blaine published his profile of Peter Dutton as a *Quarterly Essay*. This is how he described his conversation with Malcolm Turnbull during the course of the referendum campaign:

> 'As prime minister, [Malcolm Turnbull] framed the Voice as a "third chamber to parliament" and predicted that a referendum on the matter would "go down in flames." This was based on his bitter experience as the leader of Australia's republic movement. "Why would you listen to Malcolm Turnbull on referendums?" he asks now. "They're all geniuses. Let's hope they are. And I'm proved terribly wrong."

> 'Turnbull has backflipped on his previous opposition to a constitutionally enshrined advisory body. He is going to vote Yes. But he insists that No will win, due to a country with a phobia for constitutional change. And he believes this would have been the result anyway, with or without Dutton's scare campaign. ..."If it goes down, a lot of people will round on Albanese and say it's all his fault," says Turnbull. "He'll get blamed for something that was probably never winnable."'[105]

Turnbull was right all along. And many politically literate people on both sides of the referendum case knew he was.

Would it have been better for me to have remained silent, backing the government proposal from the outset at Garma and declining to comment publicly on the need for amendment to the proposed wording? I thought not, and I am still of that view. I addressed many audiences and engaged in lengthy Q&A sessions. Every audience contained three groups: the rusted on 'yes' voters; the committed 'no' voters; and the undecided. Particularly with church audiences, I thought it essential to be completely candid, outlining the complexities and the problems, before then stating my own personal choice to vote 'yes', and why. I was happy to vote yes, despite the flaws. I was prepared to admit what those flaws were. Nothing in life is perfect. No constitutional change is perfect. We had a choice between an imperfect set of words which would honour what was being sought by a significant cohort of the nation's Indigenous leaders who had proven track records of commitment to their people, and an unamended Constitution which left the issue of constitutional recognition of our First Peoples for another generation to determine. I thought the time had come for change.

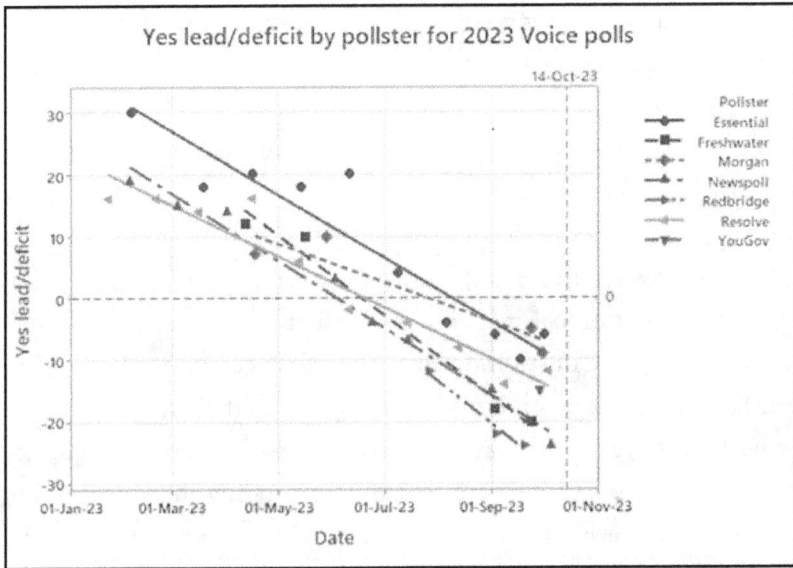

Yes lead/deficit by pollster for 2023 Voice polls

In the last few weeks of the campaign, it was clear that the referendum was lost. All the polls were going south relentlessly.[106] Some of the referendum's proponents started a narrative that failure would be due to the inherent racism of Australian society. I thought it inappropriate that such a narrative take hold. I gave three interviews (on 2, 4 and 9 October) highlighting that the likely failure of the referendum would be the result of the government's abuse of process and overbroad, insufficiently scrutinised wording of the provision.

I admire those Australians who throughout the campaign committed themselves unreservedly with their time and resources to advocating for the proposed amendment, despite the shortcomings of process and wording. Having been an advocate for Indigenous rights in the public square for the last 40 years, I thought it necessary to do all I could to improve the process and the wording. I failed, as did many others. I am sorry for the hurt caused to those who thought I should overlook the shortcomings in the hope that the public would get with the vibe, go with the flow, and vote Yes in overwhelming numbers. But that's just not the way that constitutional change has ever happened in Australia. And it won't next time, either. Buckets of money from the corporate sector in support of a worthy cause are no substitute for the hard work of getting the wording right and winning cross-party support in the parliament. Let's all have the humility to admit our mistakes, regroup, forgive the hurts, and move on, seeking the due constitutional recognition of First Australians. We won't ever amend the Constitution unless we first get most members of parliament on board, and unless we can assure the public that there is nothing to fear, and that there is no unresolved legal complexity and uncertainty. And when it comes to amending the Constitution to recognise the First Australians, there will be no point unless the key Indigenous leaders are advocating the change with one Voice. Though they were devastated by the 2023 defeat, these leaders had sufficient hope to declare in the midst of their despair: 'We have faith that the upswelling of support through this Referendum has ignited a fire for many to walk with us on our journey towards justice. Our truths have been silenced for too long.'[107] We need to kindle that fire and continue that long journey.

Having had cause to reflect on 'the bitter division of the voice debate', Professor George Williams who was a member of the Albanese government's 8 member Constitutional Expert Group, has now said: 'The nation needs a long-term approach to constitutional reform, not one focused on the short-term political cycle. The best model is a small, nonpartisan constitutional commission tasked with reviewing the Constitution and assessing reforms with the community and our political leaders. The best ideas should then be road-tested at a popular constitutional convention every 10 years before being put to the people at a referendum. If proposals ... cannot pass the gauntlet of the commission and convention, they should proceed no further.'[108] If only the expert group had proffered such advice in 2023. If only such advice had been heeded by Mr Albanese and his cabinet colleagues.

During the 1993 native title debate, Paul Keating was fond of saying, 'Good policy will be good politics'. The lesson of 2023 is that good process will yield good policy, which will produce good politics, which might then result in a popular positive referendum result. Last year, the horse fell at the first hurdle of process and then went way off track. Next time, we could all do better by following the basic rules of constitutional change.

Endnotes

1   See https://ulurustatement.org/statement-for-our-people-and-country/

2   Ibid.

3   Garratt Publishing, 2023 (3 editions, February 2023, May 2023 and July 2023).

4   University of Queensland Press, 2015.

5   This was my homily for the 28th Sunday in Ordinary Time, 15 October 2023. The readings were Isaiah 25:6-10a; Psalm 23; Philippians 4:12-14, 19-20; Matthew 22:1-14. Listen at https://soundcloud.com/frank-brennan-6/homily-151023.

6   Isaiah 25:6-10a.

7   https://www.vatican.va/content/john-paul-ii/en/speeches/1986/november/documents/hf_jp-ii_spe_19861129_aborigeni-alice-springs-australia.html

8   See https://www.theaustralian.com.au/inquirer/room-must-be-made-at-the-table-for-other-indigenous-voices/news-story/fd080462358d922a90e939e06066d5fc

9   Prime Minister's Press Conference, 15 October 2023, available at https://www.pm.gov.au/media/press-conference-parliament-house-canberra-17.

10 Note from Dan Tehan to author, 24 February 2023.

11 https://www.theaustralian.com.au/commentary/an-indigenous-voice-will-help-fight-against-endemic-disease/news-story/c7e15d11478b835129683d78529df9b3

12 *Students for Fair Admissions, Inc.* v. *President and Fellows of Harvard College*, 600 U. S. ____ (2023), Jackson J in dissent (with Sotomayor and Kagan JJ) at p. 1.

13 Ibid, p. 2.

14 Ibid, Thomas J, p. 51.

15 Ibid, Opinion of the Court, p. 16.

16 *Haaland* v *Bracken*, Opinion of the Court, 599 US __ (2023), at p. 12.

17 See https://www.skynews.com.au/australia-news/politics/it-was-always-doomed-the-voice-was-defective-from-the- beginning/video/10678e5749b292402f99beaa0c-be2ab9; https://www.youtube.com/watch?v=8R_4rQaNctQ&t=19s

18 See https://www.theguardian.com/commentisfree/2023/oct/22/australias-constitutional-history-told-us-the-voice-referendum-was-unwinnable-sadly-that-was-right-malcolm-turnbull

19 See https://ulurustatement.org/statement-for-our-people-and-country/

20 *The Swag*, Newsletter of the National Council of Priests, Summer 2023, pp. 5-6.

21 Prime Minister's Press Conference, 15 October 2023, available at https://www.pm.gov.au/media/press-conference-parliament-house-canberra-17.

22   Megan Davis, Address to the National Press Club, 9 November 2022.

23   Letter to Prime Minister Anthony Albanese, 9 November 2022, available at pp. 61-64.

24   Andrew Bragg, ABC Interview, 14 June 2023, available at https://www.andrew-bragg.com/post/interview-with-hamish-macdonald-on-rn-breakfast

25   Senate, *Hansard*, 13 June 2023, p. 64.

26   *Sydney Morning Herald*, 16 October 2023, available at https://www.smh.com.au/politics/federal/the-devil-in-the-details-inside-the-yes-campaign-s-defeat-20231010-p5eb6h.html

27   House of Representatives, *Hansard*, 23 August 1988, p. 141.

28   Senate, *Hansard*, 23 August 1988, p.63.

29   Fred Chaney, 'How the Voice will help government', *The Saturday Paper*, 15-21 July 2023.

30   Pope Francis, *Laudato Si'*, #146.

31   Pope John Paul II, Address to the Aboriginal People, Alice Springs, 29 November 1986, available at https://www.vatican.va/content/john-paul-ii/en/speeches/1986/november/documents/hf_jp-ii_spe_19861129_aborigeni-alice-springs-australia.html.

32   NATSICC, 'Not the end of the journey', 17 October 2023, available at https://melbournecatholic.org/news/not-the-end-of-the-journey-natsicc-releases-statement-on-referendum-result.

33   The readings were Exodus 22:20-26; Psalm 17; 1 Thessalonians 1:5-10; Matthew 22:34-40. Listen at https://soundcloud.com/frank-brennan-6/homily-291023.

34   See https://ulurustatement.org/statement-for-our-people-and-country/

35   https://www.smh.com.au/politics/federal/good-on-you-for-having-a-try-albanese-quizzed-about-the-voice-in-us-20231027-p5efox.html

36   See https://www.youtube.com/watch?v=8R_4rQaNctQ&t=19s

37   Michael Walzer, *Thinking Politically*, Yale University Press, 2007, p.276

38   *Legal Consequences of the Construction of a Wall in the Occupied Palestinian Territory*, International Court of Justice, *Advisory Opinion*, ICJ Reports 2004, p. 136 at para. 137 available at https://www.icj-cij.org/sites/default/files/case-related/131/131-20040709-ADV-01-00-EN.pdf

39   Judgment of Buergenthal J, para. 2 available at https://www.icj-cij.org/sites/default/files/case-related/131/131-20040709-ADV-01-05-EN.pdf

40   A/RES/ES -10/15.

41   See https://www.eurekastreet.com.au/article/lessons-from-the-referendum. An edited 3,000 version later appeared in *The Australian*, 1 March 2024 at https://www.theaustralian.com.au/inquirer/albaneses-errors-

undermined-any-hope-of-achieving-change-through-the-voice/news-story/
bddac4027d1c5c623a9124e7321fc9f3

42   Malcolm Turnbull, *A Bigger Picture*, Hardie Grant, 2020, p. 570.

43   Ibid, p. 571.

44   Referendum Council, *Final Report*, 2017, p. 2.

45   Professor Megan Davis, Pro Vice-Chancellor Indigenous, University of New South Wales, *Proof Committee Hansard*, Joint Select Committee on Constitutional Recognition relating to Aboriginal and Torres Strait Islander Peoples, Canberra, 18 September 2018, p. 5.

46   Professor Anne Twomey, 'Constitutional conventions, commissions and other constitutional reform mechanisms', *Public Law Review*, Volume 19, No. 4, December 2008, p. 309.

47   Joint Select Committee on Constitutional Recognition relating to Aboriginal and Torres Strait Islander Peoples, *Final Report*, 2018, p. 92.

48   Ibid, p. 118.

49   Anthony Albanese, Garma Address, 30 July 2022, available at https://www.pm.gov.au/media/address-garma-festival.

50   R. Ellicott, 'Indigenous Recognition: Some Issues' in *Proceedings of the 23rd Conference of the Samuel Griffith Society*, 2012, p. 80.

51   House of Representatives, *Hansard*, 22 June 2023, p. 77.

52   Ibid.

53   In *Kartinyeri* v *Commonwealth* (1998) 195 CLR 377 at pp. 382-3, Justices Hayne and Gummow had cause to consider whether the 1967 statute which was a prelude to the 1967 referendum could be used to read implied limits into the head of power contained in the constitutional change. They said: 'The text is not limited by any implication such as that contended for by the plaintiffs. This is so whether one has regard alone to the terms of the Constitution after the 1967 Act took effect or also to that statute. The circumstances surrounding the enactment of the 1967 Act, assuming regard may properly be had to them, may indicate an aspiration of the legislature and the electors to provide federal legislative powers to advance the situation of persons of the Aboriginal race. But it does not follow that this was implemented by a change to the constitutional text which was hedged by limitations unexpressed therein.' They went on to say: 'The omission in the 1967 Act of any limitation, making specific reference to the provision of "benefits" to persons of the Aboriginal race, upon the operation of the amended s 51(xxvi), is consistent with a wish of the Parliament to avoid later definitional argument in the legislature and the courts as to the scope of its legislative power. That is the effect of what was achieved.' *A fortiori*, there is no way you could refer to a second reading speech in the parliament trying to read down the scope of a constitutional amendment.

54 Mark Butler, 'An Indigenous voice will help fight against endemic disease', *The Australian*, 24 August 2023, available at https://www.theaustralian.com.au/commentary/an-indigenous-voice-will-help-fight-against-endemic-disease/news-story/c7e15d11478b835129683d78529df9b3.

55 Noel Pearson, 'A Rightful but not Separate Place', *Boyer Lecture Two*, available at https://capeyorkpartnership.org.au/noel-pearson-boyer-lecture-two/.

56 Homily for the 4th Sunday of Lent, 10 March 2024. The readings were 2 Chronicles 36:14-16,19-23; Psalm 137; Ephesians 2:4-10; John 3:14-21. Listen at https://soundcloud.com/frank-brennan-6/homily-10324

57 https://www.theaustralian.com.au/commentary/course-of-our-history-shaped-by-a-leaders-leader/news-story/70177374769a677bfaa0ca495e49373c

58 https://www.austlii.edu.au/cgi-bin/viewdoc/au/journals/IndigLawB/1997/35.html

59 https://www.afr.com/politics/federal/it-s-time-for-australia-to-break-out-of-its-timidity-keating-20240219-p5f66h

60 See https://johnmenadue.com/death-of-lowitja-odonoghue/

61 https://www.dunstan.org.au/wp-content/uploads/2020/05/Lowitja-ODonoghue-Orations-Book_Final.pdf, p. 58.

62 https://www.austlii.edu.au/cgi-bin/viewdoc/au/journals/IndigLawB/1997/35.html

63 I gave this note to Ministers Dreyfus, Burney and Gorman and discussed it with each of them on 22 March 2023. Houston Ash was present at the meeting with Dreyfus and Tim Watts at the meeting with Burney. Gorman and I met alone. On 20 March 2023, I had advised Tim Gartrell, 'I'm meeting with Burney, Dreyfus and Gorman on Wednesday and will see McCarthy on Saturday night.' At 8am on 22 March 2023, I provided Gartrell with a copy of the note observing, 'These are my talking notes for today with Linda, Patrick and Mark.' I urged Dreyfus to obtain advice from the Solicitor General on the point I raised about the need for a public servant to provide notice and sufficient information for the Voice to make an informed representation. That was never done.

64 https://www.theaustralian.com.au/commentary/benefits-of-the-voice-will-far-outweigh-risks/news-story/aa752c3d9ac7a9f4ec6d70f1fc7b872d).

65 https://www.afr.com/politics/why-bret-walker-says-voice-litigation-won-t-matter-20230313-p5crlj)

66 https://ministers.pmc.gov.au/burney/2023/media-conference-adelaide

67 Joint Select Committee on the Aboriginal and Torres Strait Islander Voice Referendum, Inquiry into the Aboriginal and Torres Strait Islander Voice Referendum, *Hansard*, 1 May 2023, pp. 21-26.

68 Frank Brennan, 'Acknowledging Indigenous Heritage a Good Beginning', The Weekend Australian, 16-17 May 2015, 16.

69 House of Representatives, *Hansard*, 31 May 2023, p. 3894.

70   See https://theconversation.com/putting-words-to-the-tune-of-indigenous-constitutional-recognition-42038

71   Joint Select Committee on Constitutional Recognition relating to Aboriginal and Torres Strait Islander Peoples, *Final Report*, 2018, pp. 91-92.

72   See https://theconversation.com/there-are-many-ways-to-achieve-indigenous-recognition-in-the-constitution-we-must-find-one-we-can-agree-on-142163

73   Frank Brennan, *An Indigenous Voice to Parliament: Considering a Constitutional Bridge*, Garratt Publishing, 2023, p.113.

74   Anthony Albanese, Media Release, 23 March 2023, available at https://www.pm.gov.au/media/next-step-towards-voice-referendum-constitutional-alteration-bill.

75   Julian Leeser proposed his amendments in the House of Representatives on 31 May 2023 (*Hansard*, p.3894). His amendments were also proposed as 'opposition amendments' in the Senate on 16 June 2023 by Senator Colbeck, the motion being negatived with no one other than Colbeck voting in support. Senator Cash, Deputy Leader of the Opposition in the Senate said: '[A]s a threshold issue, we do not believe the Voice should be enshrined in the Constitution. There is no amendment to this bill which can clear that threshold, and supporting this amendment to the bill would require us to support the idea that the Voice should be in the Constitution.' (*Hansard*, pp.2490-2). A week later, the Prime Minister told a media conference: 'I note that when the Senate passed the legislation for a referendum this year, what it did was, this week, there were no votes on any amendments put forward, none.' (see https://www.pm.gov.au/media/press-conference-parliament-house-canberra-15).

76   Schedule 1, *Constitution Alteration (Aboriginal and Torres Strait Islander Voice) 2023*.

77   See https://www.hcourt.gov.au/assets/publications/speeches/current-justices/frenchcj/frenchcj25jan10.pdf

78   See https://www.afr.com/politics/federal/voice-is-low-risk-but-high-return-20230201-p5ch8e.

79   See https://theconversation.com/politics-with-michelle-grattan-frank-brennan-on-rewording-voice-question-200442?fbclid=IwAR3NJdoZNA2FWvfl-waQZ-hZGj3jOFpCOQeMbL3KXOtwms575QBU5gy0gexI.

80   See https://www.theaustralian.com.au/commentary/parliament-will-add-flesh-to-indigenous-voice/news-story/9ead36a77c3f861a6847e2afaad76e50

81   Murray Gleeson, *Recognition in Keeping with the Constitution: A Worthwhile Project*, Uphold and Recognise, July 2019, available at https://static1.squarespace.com/static/57e8c98bbebafba4113308f7/t/623fd3c9ddee2d421effe7fd/1648350153940/Recognition+folio+A5_SinglePages.pdf

82   Stephen Gageler, 'Impact of migration law on the development of Australian administrative law', (2010) 17 *Australian Journal of Administrative Law* 92, 103

83   Ibid, pp. 104-5

84   *Plaintiff S157* v *The Commonwealth* (2003) 211 CLR 476

85   Robert French, *'Constitutional Review of Executive Decisions –Australia's US Legacy'*, John Marshall Law School – Chicago Bar Association, 25 January 2010, p. 10

86   *Plaintiff M1-2021* v *Minister for Home Affairs* [2022] HCA 17 (http://www.austlii.edu.au/cgi-bin/viewdoc/au/cases/cth/HCA/2022/17.html.

87   Ian Callinan, https://www.theaustralian.com.au/inquirer/examining-the-case-for-the-voice-an-argument-against/news-story/e30c8f2ffcbae73eaa3921e82bf174a9

88   Kenneth Hayne, https://www.abl.com.au/insights-and-news/the-more-you-look-the-less-there-is-to-see-former-high-court-judge-kenneth-hayne-dissects-and-dismisses-fearmongering-around-the-first-nations-voice/

89   Robert French and Geoffrey Lindell, 'The Voice is low risk but high return', available at https://www.afr.com/politics/federal/voice-is-low-risk-but-high-return-20230201-p5ch8e

90   https://www.theaustralian.com.au/inquirer/examining-the-case-for-the-voice-an-argument-against/news-story/e30c8f2ffcbae73eaa3921e82bf174a9

91   Robert French had communicated with me privately via an intermediary on 8 February 2023. This was my response to his observations.

92   See https://ministers.pmc.gov.au/burney/2022/communique-referendum-working-group-0)

93   https://www.afr.com/politics/federal/voice-is-low-risk-but-high-return-20230201-p5ch8e

94   see https://www.theaustralian.com.au/commentary/expert-stress-tests-show-the-voice-is-not-a-threat/news-story/a74b4d247a05fc1e2131f29acaf26e63

95   https://www.theaustralian.com.au/commentary/expect-the-courts-to-play-a-role-in-operation-of-voice/news-story/9727e5b6f674ea5c4c0b722db3e6d27c

96   https://www.pm.gov.au/media/question-and-answer-national-press-club

97   Robert French, 'Parliament will add flesh to voice skeleton', *The Australian*, 13 July 2023, available at https://www.theaustralian.com.au/commentary/parliament-will-add-flesh-to-indigenous-voice/news-story/9ead36a77c-3f861a6847e2afaad76e50.

98   (2016) HCA 29; 259 CLR 180 at 207 (83). For some insights into the present High Court's view on the need for procedural fairness, see *Disorganized Developments Pty Ltd* v *South Australia* [2023] HCA 22 (2 August 2023) in which the court had to consider the extent to which government would need to extend procedural fairness to an illegal bike gang whose property was to be subject to classification as a prescribed place. At para 54, Kiefel CJ, Gageler, Gleeson and Jagot JJ observe: 'Procedural fairness under this scheme requires reasonable notice to an owner or occupier of a proposal to declare a place a prescribed place, to give them an opportunity to supply information or make

submissions as to matters within their knowledge as an owner or occupier that may be relevant to a decision to exercise the declaration power.' A fortiori, would not a constitutional entity such as the Voice have an entitlement to procedural fairness before a public servant made a decision relating to Aboriginal and Torres Strait Islander persons especially when that decision is likely to impact distinctively on those who are Aboriginal or Torres Strait Islander?

99   Query whether Jackson here meant s.129(3).

100   See https://www.afr.com/politics/federal/the-voice-was-a-mistake-from-the-start-20240219-p5f66v

101   See https://www.afr.com/politics/federal/langton-says-keating-was-right-on-the-voice-20240220-p5f6h9

102   See https://www.theaustralian.com.au/weekend-australian-magazine/peter-garrett-on-the-failure-of-the-voice-referendum-protecting-cape-york-and-healing-old-wounds/news-story/8cbed136bbb42f3b814a24e8341eb420

103   Solicitor General, Opinion, *In The Matter of Proposed Section 129 of The Constitution*, 19 April 2023, p.5.

104   'Can the Voice be Rescued', Ben Fordham, 2GB, Sydney, 21 February 2023 available at https://www.2gb.com/can-the-voice-be-rescued-father-frank-brennan-enters-the-debate/

105   Lech Blaine, 'Bad Cop: Peter Dutton's Strongman Politics', *Quarterly Essay*, Issue 93, 2024, pp.93-4.

106   See https://theconversation.com/final-voice-polls-have-no-leading-by-sizeable-to-landslide-margins-215264

107   See https://ulurustatement.org/statement-for-our-people-and-country/

108   George Williams, 'Good ideas lost in a broken system overdue for reform', *The Weekend Australian*, 13-14 April 2024, p. 15, available at https://www.theaustralian.com.au/commentary/good-ideas-lost-in-a-broken-system-thats-overdue-for-reform/news-story/b27e4ad5eaa930dab7f15657d1102542. Williams was considering a proposal for four year terms – a proposal far less controversial, far more familiar and much less complex than the Voice.

About the Author

Fr Frank Brennan SJ AO is a Jesuit priest and superior of the Alberto Hurtado community of Jesuits in Brisbane. He was appointed a peritus at the Fifth Plenary Council of the Catholic Church in Australia. He is a Distinguished Fellow of the PM Glynn Institute at Australian Catholic University, an Adjunct Professor at the Thomas More Law School at ACU and research professor at the Australian Centre for Christianity and Culture. He was previously the CEO of Catholic Social Services Australia and Rector of Newman College at the University of Melbourne. He chaired the National Human Rights Consultation for the Rudd Government and was a member of the Turnbull Government's expert panel which conducted the Religious Freedom Review. The Morrison Government appointed him to the Voice Co-Design Senior Advisory Group to help guide the Co-Design process to develop options for an Indigenous voice to parliament.

He has previously published three books on Indigenous constitutional recognition: *Sharing the Country* (Penguin Books, two editions, 1992 and 1994); *No Small Change: The Road to Recognition for Indigenous Australia* (University of Queensland Press, 2015); and *An Indigenous Voice to Parliament: Considering a Constitutional Bridge* (Garratt Publishing, 2023, three editions). During the 2023 referendum campaign, he was asked by the Jesuit provincial to traverse the country addressing audiences wanting to know more about the proposed constitutional change. He worked closely with the National Aboriginal and Torres Strait Islander Catholic Council. John Lochowiak, the Chairperson of NATSICC provides a foreword to this book.

www.ingramcontent.com/pod-product-compliance
Lightning Source LLC
Chambersburg PA
CBHW050531270326
41926CB00015B/3169